You Can Believe!

You Can Believe!

An Introduction to the New Christianity

Grant Schnarr

Chrysalis Books

Library of Congress Cataloging-in-Publication Data

Schnarr, Grant R.
   You can believe!: an introduction to the new Christianity /
Grant R. Schnarr.
      p. cm.
Includes bibliographical references.
ISBN 0-87785-318-5
1. New Jerusalem Church--Doctrines. 2. Swedenborg, Emanuel, 1688–1772. I. Title.
BX8721.3.S33 2006
289'.4--dc22
                2005029169

Edited by Mary Lou Bertucci
Designed by Karen Connor
Typeset in Garamond by Karen Connor
Printed in the United States of America
Cover photo by Cezary Gwozdz

Chrysalis Books is an imprint of the Swedenborg Foundation, Inc. For more information, contact:

Chrysalis Books
Swedenborg Foundation
320 North Church Street
West Chester, PA 19380
info@swedenborg.com or www.swedenborg.com.

DEDICATION

When I was a young minister in the 1980s, I struggled to get a church started among young people in an old café in Rogers Park, Chicago. It was difficult work. Back in those days, I would labor all week on a sermon, hoping for a good crowd on Sunday, but often hardly anyone showed up. One particular young woman would slip in the back door of the café after I started preaching each Sunday. She would stay until the sermon was over and then dart out before anyone could talk to her. One day, when attendance was particularly low and I was about ready to give up ministry and take up some easier occupation, she stayed after the service and came over to speak with me. She told me that she was leaving Chicago and wanted me to know. She was going home to start again. "I ran away," she said, "from my home in Florida. Your talks have kept me alive and given me meaning again. I'm going back home to my family to start again. I just wanted to say thank you." She touched my hand and walked out the door. I turned away as tears instantly filled my eyes. I knew then that all the pain and disappointment of this work was worth it just for this young woman. I wished her the best. I never saw her again.

This book is dedicated to her.

CONTENTS

Introduction: Why Can't I Believe?   ix

1   Who Is God?   3

2   What Am I Doing Here?   17

3   How Can I Grow?   25

4   Am I Being Cared For?   35

5   What Is the Bible Telling Us?   43

6   Does Love Last Forever?   55

7   Is There an Afterlife?   63

8   Are We Living in the End Times?   75

9   You Can Believe!   81

Who Was Emanuel Swedenborg?   85

Bibliography   89

INTRODUCTION

Why Can't I Believe?

We live in a cynical time, especially when it comes to faith. We see religious people portrayed as misguided simpletons, while newspaper headlines reveal some spiritual leaders as charlatans. We see people kill other people in the name of religion, and we hear a common criticism time and again that religion has done more harm than good in this world. Such problems would cause anyone to pause before venturing down the road of spiritual pursuit. Many people have made a jumble of religion, and it repels us; yet somehow we know that something has been taken away from us, something precious has been lost without the guide of spiritual teachings. Our connection to the Source, to one another, to the magic and the moment, to the core of life itself has been left behind somewhere. Still, we long for belief, for hope, for the supernatural above or beyond ourselves that we can reach out to and feel, draw to ourselves and wrap ourselves in. We know that spirituality is more than religion or the blind allegiance to ignorant dogma.

It's not just the vast armies of religious zealots who have caused many of the rest of us to give pause before joining such a following. Our inability to believe is also deeply affected by Western culture, a world of consumerism, commercialism, and constant marketing propaganda that bombards us with messages that we do not have enough, that we deserve the world, that we need to put number one, ourselves, above others. Although these messages do not necessarily prevent us from seeking spiritual life, they devalue such a pursuit, as if it were nothing.

What we witness around us contributes to our lack of initiative to pursue faith. One of my friends who dropped out of the marketing profession to seek a career in a helping profession once put it this way, "I just got tired of perpetuating the illusion." The "illusion" is that spirit simply doesn't exist and so can bring no satisfaction, let alone happiness. To fill up the void of spirit, we are urged to accumulate material wealth and possessions, to live in the moment and experience any aspect of diversion that suits our pleasure, whether it hurts another or not. And on the other hand, the news sources daily recount tragic stories in which misguided religious people, through their perverted interpretations and fanatical acts in the name of religion, have turned the pursuit of spirituality either into a dangerous game of who's who in God's little book of the damned or into tragic scenes where the innocent are slaughtered as a means to fulfill some fanatical "heavenly" mission.

But these barriers stem from illusion themselves and so can be overcome. Maybe you've heard some say something like, "I'm not a religious person, but strive to be a spiritual person." There's a lot of wisdom in that saying. Can we drop our preconceived notions of religion and spirituality and start from scratch? We can.

Barriers to Belief

With the people I counsel, I find that the real barriers that stop them from believing are the ones on the inside. Oddly enough, what stops many of us from living a spiritual life is our past experience, for example, beliefs that may have been thrust upon us or the fear of having to return to a childhood belief system that made no sense or was actually hurtful. Ask yourself what stops you from pursuing spiritual belief. Are wounds from the past stopping you? That situation is very common.

Josh feels he cannot believe in God because of what he was taught about God in the past. He can't face that angry, judgmental, playground bully of a God—scary images he received as a child from zealous Sunday school teachers. He feels that he can't even approach the Deity because this is the only picture of God he has experienced.

Sharon had a bad experience with religion while growing up. Her parents took her to church every Sunday until she was 12. The parents had a falling out with the local minister. There was scandal. One day they just stopped going to church, and Sharon never knew why. Her parents just told her that they "don't do that any more." Today Sharon feels afraid that if she finds faith again it just might be taken away from her. She struggles to separate herself from her parents' arbitrary decision to cut the entire family off from religion because of their reaction to an event or to one person.

Do you have that same problem trying to separate from your parents' religion? Many do. With most it is about what was jammed down their throats when they were children—an angry, vengeful or even an uncaring God, hell as an eternal torture chamber, heaven as a cloud where dull harpists sit for eternity, nonsensical views about the inequality of the sexes, sex itself as something dirty or as a "necessary evil" for the propagation of the human race, or a belief system reduced to a set of words, dogma replacing love, fear replacing mercy, a dark and dreary view of life. Do any of these beliefs scare you away from spiritual pursuit? Do you say sometimes, "I wish I could find something to believe, but I can't go back there?"

Another barrier to belief is that many today grow up without any spiritual beliefs at all as their own parents were nonbelievers. They sense they are missing something. Bobbie says she wants so badly to believe in God but doesn't know where to start. She never had God while growing up. She wants to have a relationship with the Divine, but prayer, or even talking to God, doesn't come easily to her. She feels like the character portrayed by Paul Newman in the old classic movie *Coolhand Luke*, who sits in a church and asks, "God, are you up there? Is *anybody* there?" How can she connect? Where does she start? What should she believe that would give her a foundation from which to build her spiritual faith and life?

Do You Wish to Be Made Well?

Once Jesus was led to a man who had sat by a magical pool for thirty-eight years (John 5:8). The story was that many sick and lame people gathered around this pool because an angel would come now and then and stir the waters. The first one into the pool would be healed. Jesus came to this man, who was so lame he clearly couldn't get to the water in time, and asked him, "Do you wish to be made well?" The man said he had no one to help him, someone always beat him to the water, he couldn't get to the water in time. But Jesus knew that this man had actually given up hope of getting to the water. He had become accustomed to his debilitating condition and comfortable with it. He should have realized after several weeks that he wouldn't get to that water, but apparently he sat there most of his life. After hearing this man's excuses, Jesus looked into this man's eyes and into his soul and said, "Arise. Take up your bed, and walk." The man got right up and walked. He was healed.

Jesus' words apply to you as well, whether you are Christian or not, or don't know yet what you are or want to be. You don't need to wait to get started. You can't wait for someone else to come along and create your spiritual life for you, carrying you to the waters of belief and healing. In fact, everything you need to get started exists within you right now because God is always with you, whether you know it or not. Get up. Get started. When it comes to the injuries you may have suffered from past experience with religion, are you willing to let the past go and start again? Are you willing to let those wounds heal, and stand up for yourself and choose to believe? You can do it. If you have no experience with faith, are you willing to take the risk of learning, and stand and take that first step on the greatest adventure of your life, leading to spirit, wonder, happiness, connection, meaning, the Divine! You can do it. Arise! Take that first step. Be willing to let go of all your preconceived notions of religion, and let go of your fears of the unknown. That's step one.

Take the next step. Ask God to show you the way, even if you feel you don't know God. Open the door, and open yourself to the possibilities. The Bible says, "Ask and it will be given to you. Seek and you will find. Knock and it shall be opened. For everyone who asks receives, and whoever seeks, finds. And to the one who knocks, it shall be opened" (Matthew 7:7–8). I certainly believe this because I've experienced it a thousand times. My hope and prayer for you are that you will too.

You Can Believe

If steps one and two are letting go of the past and asking God to show you the way, step three is learning what is out there in the way of teachings that you can choose to believe. Explore the different religions of the world. What seems to fit with what your heart is telling you? What calls to your spirit, to your conscience, to your sense of what it means to live in spirit, love, and integrity? One thing I love about my church, the New Church, is that it teaches there is good in all religions and that you don't have to belong to one particular religion to get to heaven. What is in your heart makes you a spiritual person, not whatever membership card you carry in your wallet.

I have studied all the major religions of the world and love many approaches. I make my home, however, in the New Church because it gives me a foundation from which to build my faith and my life. I can believe in Jesus Christ, and I can love Buddha's teachings. I can follow the Ten Commandments in the Bible and still believe that the Great Spirit of the Native Americans lives and moves in all things. God is the same, though called different names. I encourage you to adopt this principle—that there is good in all religions—and to find what resonates within you. If something doesn't make sense, don't believe it. If something seems hurtful to your inner spirit, trust your intuition. If something seems right, adopt it, try it, grow with it. And if something challenges you to change, stay with it. You and I need to be challenged. Change is the way life works. If you're not changing, you're not growing. And if you're not growing, you're dying. Embrace the challenge to live unselfishly, to strive for something higher, better, stronger, and nobler. If you begin to do this, you will soon see and feel with your whole being that you are not alone, that there is a force for good so strong in your life that you cannot deny it. This force is gentle and loving, as if you are being carried along in a silent current toward all things good and blessed. It's there for you. Just take up that bed and start moving.

Spirituality doesn't come about without some sort of faith. Faith clothes love with a body and bolsters the ability to live a life of love. In order to believe, you have to have something to believe in. Belief gives spirituality its form. The pursuit of God and spirit is a real journey. Belief gives direction and sets forth a path for us to follow. Our belief is a roadmap to spiritual growth, happiness, God, and heaven.

In this book, I have written about my faith, what I have adopted in my life. This is what I believe and the roadmap I use. I have chosen to share it with you because I believe that it can help you immensely, just as it has helped me. I don't believe these things because someone told me to. My beliefs are not based on blind faith, superstition, dogma, tradition, or any man-made view. I believe them because they make sense to me. I've never found anything better, and I've looked. I also believe these things because I can and don't have to stop looking, learning, and growing. The ideas presented in this book are like a boat, keeping me safe over stormy seas. They are also like a boat that I can continue to fish from, for more knowledge, understanding, food for thought and for life. You may find the same thing.

This book is an introduction to the New Christianity, based on the Bible and the teachings of the eighteenth-century scientist and theologian Emanuel Swedenborg (1688–1772). Swedenborg's influence on modern religion is huge. The modern concepts of human freedom, of spiritual growth and recovery, of a loving God, of mythology, even the modern concept of heaven, can all be said to have their roots in Swedenborgian thought. This is why, perhaps, Ralph Waldo Emerson in his book *Representative Men* called Swedenborg, "a colossal soul" or why Helen Keller, in her spiritual autobiography *Light in My Darkness*, said of Swedenborg's works, "His truths are like light and sound to my eyes and ears. Whereas once I was blind, now I see."[1] John Chapman, better known to the world as Johnny Appleseed, one of the first Swedenborgian missionaries and an American folk legend, called Swedenborg's works, "Good news, right fresh from heaven."

I don't expect you to believe this about Swedenborg's theology just because Johnny Appleseed said so. I don't believe because others have. I believe because these teachings make sense to me and give me the best picture anyone ever has of the way things are and the way things ought to be.

My hope for this book is that it will do the same for you— give you something you can believe in and a foundation upon which you can build your faith.

---

1. *Light in My Darkness*, 2nd edition, edited by Ray Silverman (West Chester, Pa.: Chrysalis Books, 2000) is a revised edition of Keller's 1927 work *My Religion*, in which she explained why she accepted the teachings of Emanuel Swedenborg as her faith.

You Can Believe!

1

Who Is God?

Our relationship with God is the most important relationship we can have. Our belief (or lack of belief) in God dictates the way we view life itself. If we see God as angry and judgmental, we tend to be angry and judgmental or view others that way. If we see God as an aloof, uncaring, intellectual concept, we tend to be aloof, uncaring, intellectual people, distanced from others, living in our own world. Many whom I've counseled who have decided not to believe in God —or who have come to the conclusion that, if there is a God, he's not doing a very good job—often suffer anger, disappointment, and hurt. What they were taught about God never measured up in their lives. He didn't seem to be there for them or for others. This reaction adds to a sense of isolation and disappointment about life in general. But being angry at God doesn't alleviate our pain, and rejecting him doesn't make our problems go away.

The real problem for most of us is that there are, indeed, many unhealthy and hurtful ideas about God being passed on. Much of what is taught about God is myth, nonsensical and manipulative, such as that he is aloof, angry, judgmental, inconsistent, impersonal, neglectful, or inept. To begin to build a helpful and genuine concept of God in our lives, we must first let go of the old concepts that prevent us from having a meaningful and life-giving relationship with our Creator.

From my experience in working to help people gain a healthier view, I have come to see the view of the Divine as an angry, judgmental bully as being the most destructive. We may never express that idea out loud, but we often think it. The Old Testament's picture of God confirms this for us, as he blasts the enemies of the Israelites or causes death among his own people who have turned away from him. Even Moses has to talk God out of killing people from time to time. God looks more like a demented, one-dimensional, comic-book character than any divinely compassionate source of life and love. The picture painted in the Old Testament is one of an angry father who warns his child, "Do this and live! Do that and die." That tone alone is enough to scare off many of us.

However, we don't have to be afraid. The teachings of the New Church, given through visionary insights of Emanuel Swedenborg, offer a new and commonsense explanation. There is a way of looking at this ancient picture of God that makes sense to today's believers.

The old picture is a reflection of humanity at that time, the way people of that age saw God in their child-like way. When they turned away from God, they saw him as angry and vengeful, a reflection of their human rulers. Also the Children of Israel acted like "children" who put themselves in such great peril that the only directives they would respond to were strong warnings of danger. In modern terms, God appeared as the parent who would continually see his children sticking their fingers in light sockets and playing tag in the busy streets. He constantly scolded them that they were going to get hurt or die if they didn't stop. The nature of the Children of Israel, and all people at that time, was to believe that God was angry all the time. But this was just an appearance.

The truth is that sometimes God appears like that to us today, when we act like children, do something wrong, and mess up our own lives. I know for me it's easy to believe that God punishes me when I do wrong or that he must be angry at me when I go against what I know is right. That's the child in me. When I reflect more rationally, I realize that this is my issue, not God's. God doesn't dislike me or anyone else. In fact, he doesn't punish us. We punish ourselves.

God Is Love

We've heard it a hundred times, seen it on bumper stickers, even on billboards: "God is Love." We read the words, but do we believe the message? It can be confusing. Sometimes the same people who exhort us to believe that God is love turn around and tell us that, if we don't belong to their religion, we're going to be sent to hell; or that if we continue to live in sin, we will surely bring down God's wrath upon us. Most traditional Christian churches teach that Jesus came to earth to appease the anger of the Father and to save us. Who is Jesus saving us from? Well, in essence, God! That can't be right! Which is it? Is God love or is God vengeance? How can he be both? And if he is both, what kind of God do we have up there running things? It's not a very pleasant picture.

What is the essence of God? Many people can agree that he is the beginning and the end, the source, reality, life itself. All spirit in all people and things, all that is animate, growing, living, breathing, existing, all things that have being, essence, and form owe their existence and subsistence to the source, the origin of life and creation itself—God. So, he isn't a comic-book character.

God is bigger than that: he is the immeasurable fountain of life. We can also say that this life comes forth from God's love. As Swedenborg said in *Divine Love and Wisdom* §1, "Love is our life."[1] In fact, love is the life of all things. This love comes

---

1. As is customary in Swedenborgian studies, the numbers following titles refer to paragraph or section numbers, which are uniform in all editions, rather than to page numbers.

forth in its very essence as endeavor, the force of life moving forward to fulfill its end. Love directs all things, from the love of life and living to a love of sharing and giving, from the warmth in each beating heart to the warmth of a tender embrace. All that love is life and all that life is God. God is life, and God is love.

Here's one insight that can help immensely if you can let go of old ideas about God. God condemns no one to misery or to hell; in fact, he *cannot* condemn us. Can you believe that? God can't condemn us, hate us, give up on us, disapprove of us, or ever reject us. Love cannot cease from loving. Love creates and does not destroy. Love encourages and supports. Love does not condemn and turn away. God not only loves us but is constantly there to lift us up and bring us to a better place than we could bring ourselves. God is our greatest supporter, our biggest fan, our ideal parent, mentor, guardian, and friend. Yes, he is our friend and at the same time is the omniscient, omnipresent, omnipotent Creator and Sustainer of the universe.

But what about hell and misery? They are real. But they do not originate in God. We create our own hell. We create our own misery when we turn away from the source of life and love. I know that, when I turn away from being a loving, trusting, helpful person to being a selfish, fearful, self-serving person—a situation that, unfortunately, happens from time to time—I put myself through hell in the process. I can't be happy if I cut myself off from love, from trust in a higher power, and from a connection to others. I feel isolated, fearful, empty, and completely dissatisfied. That's hell for me. You know what I am talking about because it is the human experience. We create our own hell on earth.

I further believe that the hell we create follows us after death and that hell is a place where spirits go who don't want heaven and the love and fellowship heaven has to offer. God doesn't send us to hell. He loves us so much that he lets us go there if that's what we choose, but it's not his hell for us; it's our hell for ourselves. Later in this book, in chapter 7, I'll discuss why anyone would want to choose hell rather than heaven.

Can you come to accept this proposition? God is real because he is life itself. He is not distant but present in your life. God does not look upon you with any feeling other than love. He works constantly for your welfare but only in connection with your own choices and freedom. God's ways are not always our ways, as the Bible says (Isaiah 55:8), but God's ways are good and always lead to good. God cares, always. God loves you. Hear it this time: God loves you. Believe it: *God loves you.*

God Is Divinely Human

The Bible starts out in Genesis by saying, "So God created humankind in his image, in the image of God he created them; male and female he created them (Genesis 1:27). We humans are created in the image of God. We are human because God is human. Humanity is male and female, and the wonderful and complementary characteristics of each gender are in the image of God. In the ancient world, God was seen as a father for a variety of reasons, including ancient people's seeing God through their own patriarchal culture. It is customary in Christianity to refer to God as male because God came into the world as Jesus Christ. I honor this image of Jesus and refer to Jesus Christ, whom I revere as my Lord and my God, as my Heavenly Father. Jesus even teaches us to do this in his prayer, "Our Father in heaven . . . ." (Matthew 6:9).

However, sometimes this patriarchal view has been taken to such an extreme that theologians have claimed that God in essence is male and have made it very hard for some people to connect with him. This is another false notion—that God, in essence, is male. God takes a masculine form as Jesus Christ, but his essence transcends gender. God is Divine Love, and this love is expressed through Divine Wisdom. Love is the essence; wisdom is the form. Neither of these is male or female, but the feminine and masculine creations come from these, and both reflect the essence of God.

The image of Jesus Christ as God in human form plays not only an important but a critical role for humankind. Jesus Christ is the embodiment of the Divine in human form; as the Apostle Paul said, "For in him the whole fullness of deity dwells bodily" (Colossians 2:9). In Jesus we see the loving tenderness, the gentleness (and appropriate firmness), the guidance, the love, the healing, and the forgiveness of the Divine. In him we see God, even as Jesus himself said to Philip, "Whoever has seen me has seen the Father" (John 14:9). What Jesus gave us was a visible and human picture of God.

Consider words such as these:

> "Let the little children come to me, and do not stop them; for it is to such as these that the kingdom of heaven belongs."   Matthew 19:13

> Peace I leave with you; my peace I give to you. . . . Do not let your hearts be troubled, and do not let them be afraid.   John 14:27

> Come to me, all that are weary and are carrying heavy burdens, and I will give you rest.   Matthew 11:28

These are all invitations to Jesus' loving embrace. How does this compare to connecting to an invisible God or to life itself? It's impossible to have a personal relationship with an invisible and unknowable life force. But to know this same invisible life force in Jesus Christ, both divine and human, *is* possible. Through the Divine Humanity of Jesus Christ, the Divine is at once visible, approachable, and accessible. Swedenborg beautifully illustrates this point:

> Union with an invisible God is like union of the sight of the eye with the expanse of the universe, the bounds of which are not to be seen. Or it is like looking out into the middle of the ocean, when the gaze falls on air and sea and is frustrated. But union with a visible God is like seeing a man in the air or on the sea opening his arms and inviting you into his embrace.
>
> *True Christian Religion* §787

It all boils down to the fact that you can have a personal relationship with God through Jesus Christ, because the invisible Source of Life and Love is made visible in Jesus Christ.

One God

All the biblical prophecies point to a time when God would take on a human form and come to earth. Some of the most beautiful prophecies are found in Isaiah:

> It will be said on that day,
>   Lo, this is our God; we have waited for him, so that
>   he might save us.
>   This is the Lord for whom we have waited;
>   let us be glad and rejoice in his salvation.
>   For the hand of the Lord will rest on this mountain.
>
> Isaiah 25:9

> See, the Lord God comes with might,
>   and his arm rules with him;
> his reward is with him,
>   and his recompense before him.

He will feed his flock like a shepherd;
    he will gather the lambs in his arms,
and carry them in his bosom,
    and gently lead the mother sheep.

Isaiah 40:10–11

Therefore, the Lord himself will give you a sign. Look,
the young woman is with child and shall bear a son,
and shall name him Immanuel [literally, "God-with-us"]

Isaiah 7:14

Jesus himself confirms his divine nature and origin again and again in the Gospels, by uttering such sayings as, "The Father and I are one" (John 10:30), "Whoever has seen me has seen the Father" (John 14:9), and this striking passage, "Before Abraham was, I am" [literally, Jehovah] (John 8:58). By calling himself the "I AM," he was referring back to original Old Testament name of God first given to Moses at the burning bush when God says, "Thus you shall say to the Israelites, 'I AM [Jehovah] has sent me to you'" (Exodus 3:14). Many of the disciples end up recognizing this, even doubting Thomas, who recognized this divinity and responded to Jesus, "My Lord and my God" (John 20:28).

Many Christian churches teach that Jesus is somehow both God and human, but this is often confused by the traditional notion of the Trinity. Many of my friends brought up in traditional Christian settings have recounted to me how frustrating it was attending a church school or Sunday school as a child, asking how the divine Trinity of the Father, Son, and Holy Spirit works, and not getting an answer. It's a good question. How are these three entities spoken of in the Bible at the same time one entity or one God? The answer that my friends received from teachers was, "It's a mystery of faith" or "You shouldn't ask such questions."

Were you an inquisitive child? Did you receive that kind of response when you asked the tough questions? One gets the feeling after hearing that evasion enough times that the true answer might be that the whole traditional theory of the Trinity just doesn't work. The question of how there can be a trinity of three persons but only one God cannot be answered because the traditional view of that Trinity is flawed.

We know there is only one God. There can be only one source of life, one source of love, one creator, one savior. Even Jehovah in the Old Testament says, "Before me no god was formed, nor shall there be any after me. I, I am the LORD, and besides me there is no savior" (Isaiah 43:10–11). This passage alone begs the question. If there are, indeed, three persons in God and Jesus is standing next to Jehovah when he made this comment, was Jehovah lying to his people? After all, every biblical scholar knows that Jesus is equated with the concept of the savior. The very name Jesus means "Jehovah saves." This is another flawed idea that has pushed people away from traditional Christianity. To picture three separate individuals up in heaven running the show, once again, turns the whole concept of God into a cartoon with three superheroes who are all somehow God.

The Trinity Explained

The explanation of the Trinity given by Swedenborg for what he called the birth of a "New Christianity" makes much more sense. The Trinity of the Father, Son, and Holy Spirit is symbolic. Each of these symbolizes a different aspect of the one God. The "Father" symbolizes the invisible I AM we have spoken about, the innermost powerful creative force of God— God's soul. The "Son" is a symbol of the body of God, how this invisible life force appears to humanity. Jesus said:

Whoever sees me sees him who sent me   (John 12:45)

If you know me, you will know my Father also. From now on you do know him and have seen him
(John 14:7–9)

Do you not believe that I am in the Father and the Father is in me? The words that I say to you I do not speak on my own; but the Father who dwells in me does his works.   (John 14:10)

Moreover, the "Holy Spirit" is not a separate being that is sent forth to do God's bidding, but is rather God's influence in people's minds and hearts. When Jesus said to his disciples, "Receive the Holy Spirit" (John 20:22), he shared with them his own spirit of love and truth.

Doesn't this make sense? We know instinctively that there is one God, one source of life and love. Jesus isn't separate from this source. Jesus *is* this source in human form. His spirit isn't some strange ghostly being. It is his spirit that he breathes into us. And so, in Jesus, we do find the "fullness of the godhead bodily" as Paul said. We can worship the Lord God Jesus Christ, as the one God, in whom is a divine trinity of soul, body, and influence, represented by these different names in the New Testament. This can make a powerful difference in your belief in God.

Why God Came to Earth as Jesus Christ

We often hear that Jesus came to redeem us and to save us from our sins. But did you ever wonder what that actually means? It can't possibly mean that he came to earth to take away our own responsibility for ourselves. He didn't come here to appease the wrath of his Father or to buy back our salvation by his death. That's the simplified version of the story presented by church leaders over the centuries. It is neither accurate nor true to what is portrayed in the Bible. God "bowed the heavens" (Psalm 18:9) and came to earth not to take away our freedoms of thought, choice, and action, but to restore them.

God created the human race as objects and receivers of his love. We were created for no other reason than to be able to receive God's love into ourselves and, with it, all the blessedness and joy of that love as we express it in our lives. God's love comes to fullness through us when we receive it and return it back to him through acts of kindness and compassion to one another and through worship and love of God. But in order for every human being to love God freely and choose to express that love, we had to be free to reject it. God couldn't just create robots that would mimic love. That wouldn't be real love. God created real people, in his image and likeness, who could freely choose to fill their lives with his goodness and express that goodness in all things. But at the same time, he created us with the choice to turn away, to reject that goodness, or to twist the inflowing life and love of God into selfishness and hurt.

Over the centuries, people did just this. As they confirmed themselves into more evil and selfish acts, many chose a hellish life. The immensity and the power of hell grew and the influence of evil grew in the minds and hearts of all people. Darkness and spiritual confusion reigned. Religion and spirituality, which in its purest form is a beautiful and sacred outlook and approach to life, became reduced to fables and formulas. Instead of seeing God reflected in nature, for instance, people began to worship nature as God. Instead of focusing on the life of spirituality, religious practice became one of animal sacrifice, repeating meaningless chants, giving prescribed payments to religious leaders to buy salvation, and so many other perversions of spiritual practice that true spiritual life was not easily found. The power of evil was so great that people were losing their freedom to receive God's love and to follow a path of love and spirit. And the day there would be no more love and spirit in the world would be the day that humankind would cease to exist, for life itself would be extinguished.

Something had to be done. God couldn't just wipe out hell and the influence of evil. Hell is made up of people who have freely chosen not to follow the path of love. Not to allow us to choose the wrong path if we so wish would make the whole concept of human freedom a joke. And besides, God loves even those who turn away from him. God couldn't just come to earth as he is in his essence, either. That would be like the sun's approaching earth. We'd be overwhelmed by his presence, and our freedom to choose would be rendered useless because we'd be overawed by the Divine. The only way God could confront the power of hell and darkness was to take on a human form and confront this darkness just like every other person on this earth—as a human being who must struggle and make choices.

By taking on a human nature from Mary, who was as vulnerable to the power of evil as anyone else, God could be tempted. In fact, the life of Jesus Christ is one of continual inner temptation and battle against evil. The human part of Jesus felt as alone and frail as we do. He wasn't always conscious of the Divine within him. That is how he could be tempted, by feeling cut off from his divine essence. And so we see in the story of Jesus in the New Testament many times when the human part of him prays to the "father" for help or calls out to God or speaks of God as being someone apart from himself. This was the human part of Jesus struggling against doubt, darkness, and evil. But as he grew and gained victory over these dark forces in his own mind and heart, he became more aware of the divine nature within him, and he became one with it, as we see when he speaks of being one with the Father, claiming,

"I am the way, the truth, and the life" (John 14:6). By allowing himself to be attacked by the hells and overcoming their attack through victory in temptation, culminating with his ultimate temptation on the cross, God through his humanity defeated hell, thrusting it back into its place and restoring freedom to humankind once again.

When Jesus hung on the cross during his last temptation, he said, "It is finished," just before his spirit left this world to return to the Father. The mission was accomplished. As he left his earthly body and rose from the dead, Jesus Christ became one with the Father, so that there were not two persons but one Divinely Human God, who was now to be known and worshiped as the Lord God Jesus Christ. Right before his final ascension, Jesus said, "All authority in heaven and on earth has been given to me" (Matthew 28:18), which is to say that now we can have a powerful relationship with God through his humanity. At the very end of the last chapter of the Bible, Jesus proclaims, "I am the Alpha and the Omega, the first and the last, the beginning and the end. . . . I am the root and descendant of David, the bright morning star" (Rev. 22:12; 16), proclaiming both his divinity and his humanity, as the one God of heaven and earth.

Knowing that God came to earth and breathed the same air we breathe, that he walked the same earth and felt the same wind on his face, and at the same time that he struggled with the same demons we struggle with, felt the same internal and external bruises and hurts that we feel, endured the worst temptations that we can endure assures us that God knows us inside and out. God knows what we suffer because he has suffered too. He feels our pain because it is and was and always will be his pain too. God can lift us up, always, and comfort us and fill us with happiness and even joy because he himself struggled against and overcame the power of hell and death. Because God did, we can too, with his power and with his help. That's a powerful image: someone who created us, and then became one of us to save us.

The key to understanding and having a relationship with God lies in using our God-given rationality. When we hear an idea about the Divine being put forth, we should ask if that makes sense. What I find refreshing about the New Church view of God is that I can be a Christian without buying all that non-sense about an angry God, about comic-book images of three separate persons in one source of life, or about Jesus somehow taking me off the hook for my own life some two thousand years ago. Rather I can embrace a wonderful, human picture of the Lord Jesus as my God and accept those beautiful teachings about love and forgiveness, about hope and promised joy, about spirit and life, without misgivings. I don't have to throw it all out to make sense of God. I just need to see it in a new and true light. That makes a big difference to me. It may for you as well.

2

What Am I Doing Here?

Who am I? Why am I here? What am I supposed to be doing while I'm here? These are important questions each one of us asks ourselves many times during our lifetime. We ask questions such as these as we gaze at the immense heavens above us on a warm summer night or feel the painful core of our existence during particular life struggles or witness the birth of a child or the death of one whom we love. What is this life all about?

Why Are We Here?

Why *are* we here? It's a good question. I've heard a lot of theories on the subject. Some say we are here simply by accident. They say our consciousness, our existence, our lives are the product of a chance occurrence in the universe. We are said to be products of the big bang at the beginning of creation, which leaves us as perhaps the "stuff that stars are made of" but, really, so what? What's the purpose? Do you feel you are here, consciously breathing, gazing at this bright world, sensing all there is around you, simply by accident? I can't buy that. You may remember Descartes' famous assertion, "I think; therefore, I am." I like to take that reasoning a step further for myself: "And if I am, I am for a reason." The wonder of creation alone is enough to tell me this is so.

But it's not just the wonder of creation that leads me to believe there's more to this existence than sheer coincidence. I can close my eyes and feel it in my heart, in my spirit: the reality of love, pain, and bliss, the wonder of the unknown, and the fact that I can sense the sacred whisper to me in no uncertain terms that life is important, that I am important, so important that everything has meaning deeper than I can fathom.

Some religious authorities say that we were created for the greater glory of God, that we are here to honor God through obedience and service to him. This sounds interesting on the surface: does God need our affirmation to boost his self-esteem? Granted every religion says we should serve God, but is this because God desires people to make him look good or feel better about himself? I think not. We can serve God, and we can glorify God by our life in this world; but neither is the ultimate end of creation. The reason we are here is much more satisfying and personally meaningful than that. We were created for no other reason than to be recipients of God's love.

Love desires someone to love and to have that love returned in kind. God, being love itself, created us as partners in a loving relationship. We were created to freely receive God's love, to open our minds and hearts to all the blessings that love brings, and to open our lives so that love flows into us and through us to others. When we live in accordance with God's plan, we are filled with happiness that grows as we grow. We were created as objects and receiving vessels of God's love.

Isn't that wonderful to know? We were created by love itself. When God created each of us and breathed into our spirits the breath of life, he rejoiced. He still rejoices today, every moment of the day, and every moment of a moment. So when we ask, "Why am I here?" we can answer, "Because I'm special, someone important, worth loving. I'm here because God wanted me to be here. He created me so that I could live and soak in all the joy and beauty around me, so that I can bask in the warmth of that love, take it into the depths of my heart, and bring it out in all its glory to share with others!" What an adventure! What a pleasure!

The idea that each of us is created as objects of God's love is beautiful in its simplicity. Yet we may find this notion brings up new questions. If I am an object of love, why do I not always feel that love? If I am such a noble creation of God, why do I often reject love and embrace anger, resentment, even hate? Is life supposed to be a party that I somehow keep ruining? I have heard many theories by all sorts of self-help professionals and spiritual leaders about why we do what we do and many suggestions about what we should be doing. Some have said that we are all evil, damned to hell, and that we are the lowest of life forms. We are told that we must beg for God's mercy and can be saved from our sins simply by expressing belief. I have also heard the opposite preached by many New Age gurus. A particularly appealing notion is that we are all intrinsically good, each containing a spark of the Divine. In fact, some people say, we can become divine through rejecting the appearance of evil and embracing our inherent goodness. But I can't see that either of these extreme beliefs makes much sense. One thing I always ask myself when considering the verity of such ideas is, "Does this notion lead to good?" Jesus said, "Thus you will know them by their fruits" (Matthew 7:20). What kind of fruits do these ideas produce?

We Are Neither Completely Evil Nor Completely Good

The notion that humankind has sinned and that we are all damned for all time to eternal punishment is quite a gloomy, hopeless, and fearful thought. It leads to debilitating guilt and also harsh judgment on ourselves and others. When you look into a newborn's eyes or share a smile with a little child, can you have any feeling inside that this child is evil and destined for hell? If you can, might I suggest therapy? God doesn't create little children for hell. God creates all for heaven. We are not demonic beings in need of a miracle to save us. It can be true, however, that an individual is totally evil because that person has chosen to be apart from God. That makes sense. If we can imagine ourselves completely cut off from the attributes of God, such as goodness, mercy, and love, then surely, all that is left is evil. Take away what is good, and only evil remains. However, while we walk this earth, we are never completely separated from God. Swedenborg poetically illustrates this in *True Christian Religion* §70: "The absence of God from man is no more possible than the absence of the sun from the earth." God works within us to open our hearts to his goodness and love, which flow through us.

We do have tendencies toward evil, but there is a big difference between having tendencies toward evil and actually being evil. Each of us knows the darker side of our soul, those destructive tendencies and impulses within us. We know our own human potential for evil. But tendencies toward evil do not become truly evil until they are acted upon; then we make these tendencies realities in our life. If we grasp those tendencies to fill ourselves with anger and rage, to cultivate a resentful attitude toward others, to be selfish rather than loving, these evils become our own. They then are no longer tendencies but attributes of our life. The more we love these destructive im-pulses and act upon them, the more we make them our nature. We become what we love and do.

On the other hand, it is very appealing to believe that we are completely whole beings perfectly aligned with our God and creation. Think about how wonderful that concept can be, especially in letting us release the guilt and stop fighting to do the right thing. The one problem I find with the idea that we are totally good is that I know I'm not. I come from a long line of Germanic marauders. Part of me wants to plunder and pillage every small town and city in the world and become the supreme ruler of the universe. I'm sunk without help from the Lord to balance me out. Truthfully, every one of us is inclined to evils of every kind. I'm not alone in my inclinations toward depravity. Left to ourselves and our tendencies toward evil, we'd dive headfirst into evils of every kind. To think that we are completely good and must embrace our entire nature is not only naive but dangerous. I have worked with people who have decided to embrace the dark side, to stop hiding "the real me" from the public, to leave all responsibility to others behind, walking out the door proclaiming, "It's my turn now!" I've seen attitudes such as these create incredible pain in families, in love relationships, and for the individuals themselves. The denial of our destructive nature is dangerous because we come into denial of the harmful results of our actions. We deny evil, and so it stays in the shadows and manipulates us like puppets.

The truth is that we are intrinsically neither good nor evil. We are, at our core, free choice. We can choose evil or good, and we do choose these every day. We can choose to follow those destructive impulses that urge us to act in selfish and destructive ways, or we can choose to act from goodness and love that God instills into our hearts. Swedenborg describes us as vessels that receive influence from the spiritual world. We can open these vessels toward heaven or toward hell and receive the influences these offer us on a spiritual level. In modern terms, we are like a radio receiving signals, and we transmit these signals through us and out into the world around us. But where do we tune in? What music are we listening to, dancing our lives to, making our own, broadcasting to the world? Through our choices every day we form our character, what Swedenborg calls our "ruling love," which is either predominately good or evil, leading us to either heavenly or hellish lives. We choose how to respond to spiritual influences, and we choose what we wish to make our own. Therefore, we choose what we wish to become.

God gives us the freedom to make the wrong choices if that is the way our heart truly goes. We can choose to live a self-centered, hardened life, devoid of care for others, intent on following our own desires. In so choosing, we choose to live a hellish life on this earth and also choose hell as our eternal home. Hell, you see, is not a place of eternal punishment, of fire and brimstone; it is merely a place where power-mad, deluded, hate-filled spirits live.

But let me be clear about one thing: God created us to love and bless us—and not just for this world but for eternity. This earthly life is like our spiritual womb, where we are molded and formed before birth into eternity. Each of us is created for heaven, to spend a lifetime preparing for heaven, and forming our lives into heavenly lives full of goodness and love. This makes our decisions very important. If we do nothing and allow our more destructive tendencies to dominate us, we drift toward a hellish life. God allows us to reject the happiness of heaven for the unhappiness of hell if we choose. If we consciously turn from those destructive influences and tendencies, look to God for help in lifting us into a higher state of love and being, we grow toward heaven. This is what God wants for every one of us.

The good news is that life can be a positive experience. Each of us was placed here by a loving God who supports us and is ready to fill us with all the happiness we are willing to receive. Not all is automatically bliss. We all have tendencies inside that, if acted upon, will shut off that connection to the Divine and open up hellish doors of pain and hurt in our lives. We all make mistakes, and we all choose both evil and good on our life journey. But we are free, free to turn away from the destructive to what is truly loving and blessed.

Your life is an opportunity to make yourself what you want to be for eternity. Choose the path that leads to happiness and spiritual life. This is the path that God has chosen for you and why you were created.

> I keep the LORD always before me;
> because he is at my right hand, I shall not be moved.
> Therefore my heart is glad, and my soul rejoices;
> my body also rests secure.
> For you do not give me up to Sheol,
> or let your faithful one see the Pit.
> You show me the path of life.
> In your presence there is fullness of joy;
> in your right hand are pleasures forevermore.
>
> Psalm 16:8–11

3

How Can I Grow?

God put us here for a purpose: to be blessed by his love. This happens when we open up our hearts and minds to that love and live the life of love in all we do. When we do this, we experience all the happiness, contentment, and joy that the universe has to offer. We find fulfillment and deep peace and also experience incredible vitality. We feel alive and new. This is what Jesus meant by being born again. Our lives become new and glorious in every way.

Rebirth doesn't happen instantaneously. Jesus said, "You must be born again" (John 3:7); some have interpreted this to mean that we must accept a certain faith and that, when we do this, we will be instantly reborn. You may have been asked by a "born-again" Christian, "Are you saved?" I have always found this a peculiar statement. Are we saved or reborn by simply confessing a certain belief system? Are we suddenly made new by one dramatic event in our lives? Reason and common sense say that this is not the case. Rebirth isn't some instant, magic formula. It is not a product one buys off the shelf, uses once, and gains miraculous results. Spiritual growth is a process. Being "born again" is a process that takes a lifetime of decisions, reflections, personal revelations, actions, reactions, and living! As a matter of fact, rebirth is a lifetime of spiritual growth. As this growth continues, we find that we are becoming new beings. All things become new to us, and wonderfully fulfilling, exciting and spiritual, even as Jesus promised, "See, I am making all things new" (Rev. 21:5).

Growth is our destiny, if we choose. However, there are barriers to making this choice. We know that we have selfish tendencies that prevent us from loving. We know we can be very self-centered and even hurtful sometimes. These destructive tendencies, when acted upon, keep us from being one with God and receiving God's gift of love and its happiness. They prevent us from growing and from being what God envisions us to be. They also hurt us and others. If we want to grow spiritually and as whole human beings, we must confront this destructive part of our nature, admit that it is present in us, ask God to help us, and begin a new life. This is the process and the path to rebirth.

The Formula for Growth

If you are familiar with the many programs of recovery that use a twelve-step model, you are also familiar with the path to spiritual growth as presented in Swedenborg's teachings. Though Swedenborg compresses these steps into a handful rather than the familiar twelve steps to recovery, the overall process is the same.[1] The path to spiritual growth involves (1) undergoing self-examination, (2) recognizing and acknowledging one's destructive patterns or outright evils, (3) turning to God for help, and (4) beginning a new life. Swedenborg adds that we shouldn't try to take on all of our destructive behaviors at once, but pick one and focus on that, and then another, and another. Our behavior implies we are changing ourselves, but we must recognize that God is working through

---

1. Bill Wilson, the creator of the twelve steps for Alcoholics Anonymous, was introduced to Swedenborg's teaching by his wife Lois Burnham, daughter of a Swedenborgian scholar. Also, two foundational sources for Bill's work were William James, another son of a Swedenborgian scholar, and Carl Jung, who studied Swedenborg and quotes him throughout his works.

us and pulling us out of our own dysfunction, lifting us to new ground. While the first efforts in spiritual growth concentrate on removing our barriers to growth, the result is a life of love and useful service.

Let's look at each of these steps with a little more focus.

(1) Undergoing Self-Examination

You have heard the old saying, "Know thyself." Self-awareness is the first step in spiritual growth. Through self-examination, or what people in recovery call a "fearless moral inventory," a person becomes aware of and thus able to overcome destructive tendencies and behaviors, which block the way to spirituality. I like to think of it as weeding a garden. Every once in a while a gardener opts to take a good look at the garden to see what is growing there. In order for the good fruit to grow, the weeds and other noxious plants must be removed. The focus is on the negative, in the sense that the gardener needs to look for and discover the malignant growth that will choke out the good fruit. But the outcome is positive when the weeds are uprooted and the good fruit is given the opportunity to grow freely and ripen.

A comprehensive self-examination or personal inventory is not something we should do every day. This would be discouraging, to say the least. An annual review, or at the most, twice a year, provides plenty of opportunity to discover our shortcomings and areas for improvement. This once-a-year inventory should be a time of personal meditation and reflection. Write down what you notice about yourself. Get a reality check about what you have discovered by confiding in a good friend you can trust. Ask God to give you the courage to see the whole picture of yourself, the good, the bad, the ugly, as well as the beautiful, the brilliant, and the blessed. Look at the whole you. This is the proactive approach. Swedenborg also says that, if you can't do this, there is an "easier" approach, but it is not as proactive. That approach is to live our lives with some degree of awareness. When something goes wrong and we notice that a shortcoming or a terrible dysfunction or out-and-out evil impulse or deed has got the best of us, we should recognize it, admit that it is there, and pray to God to remove it. If we do this when these spiritual weeds, as it were, show up, then we can keep that garden growing. However, it's more proactive and efficient to look at the whole once in awhile.

(2) Recognizing and Admitting the Problem

It's not just enough to see a problem. We have to acknowledge and take responsibility for it. Otherwise, there is no hope of its going away. Have you ever had one of those insights that you are doing something for all the wrong reasons, but you are afraid to admit it to your spouse or your children? Sometimes it's hard to admit wrongs to ourselves as well. The temptation is just to say, "Well, that's the way I am." But that simply doesn't work if the way we are is selfish or hurtful. Growth can't happen if we don't admit we need to change. When we see something we need to change, can we confess to ourselves, "I was wrong. I hurt someone. This isn't good," or something like that? It makes a big difference. Suddenly we open the door and let the light shine in on our lesser nature. With the light comes the divine aid to cure our inner ills, to bring relief, a change of heart, a new love, and a new way. This type of confession to ourselves and to God makes us humble and opens us up for healing.

It's as simple as that. Confession to others is not necessary for spiritual growth, but this too can help. It can relieve the conscience and provide a sense of relief; you can see that maybe you are not so different from others after all. But if you do decide to confess your faults to others, please find a professional, such as minister, priest, therapist, life-coach, or at least a trusted confidant. Don't open yourself up to someone who can't handle the confession or who can't hold you in his or her confidence and care.

(3) Turning to God

Turning to God is crucial. We need a power greater than ourselves to help us rise above the more animalistic self and become spiritual. God, as the source of all love and wisdom, is the key to growth and spiritual prosperity. People in recovery call this step turning their will and life over to God and asking God to remove their shortcomings.

It is amazing what God can do. Jesus said that you can move a mountain if you really trust in God. That mountain can be piles of self-doubt, guilt, anger, resentment, lust, fear, or greed. It doesn't matter; with God all things are possible. If we turn to the source of power itself, that power will move those mountains and replace our troubles with peace. It may not happen all at once or in the way we expect, but it will happen. I've seen it. I've felt it. I'm sure you have too, when really overcome by some problem. God can come through.

(4) Beginning a New Life

The new life is a result of turning our will and life over to God, not once, but every day and every moment of the day. We recognize that it is God who changes us, through mercy and grace. I love that word *grace*. It means so much. It means beauty, elegance, mercy, goodwill, helpfulness, and a favor given freely, with no strings attached. It is but for the grace of God that we live and grow. Everything we have is from God, every breath we take. God's grace is his very presence lifting us up constantly toward all that is blessed. But this doesn't mean we do nothing. We can't just stand there, with our mouths open, arms hanging down, waiting for God to change us. We must act. Swedenborg says that we must act, "as if by ourselves" but fully acknowledging that all power and ability to change is from God.

I am reminded of the story of the Apostle Peter walking on the water to come to Jesus. It was through Jesus' power that Peter was held up in the storm, saved from the wind and waves, but Peter still had to walk. We need to take action to change our lives and rely on God's power to keep us afloat in the storms. We can do it, with God's help.

Growing Pains

All growth entails some sort of discomfort and even pain. Any arborist knows that pruning a tree can help it grow, even though the pruning may not be the most pleasant experience for the tree. Adolescents go through physical pain and discomfort as they grow. They go through emotional discomfort and pain too, as they seek to discover who they are and what gifts they can bring to this world. Anyone who is working to keep physically fit knows it's work. We know the old adage, "No pain, no gain."

Now, I could tell you that spiritual growth is different, that you don't have to go through anything difficult to become happy, or that heaven is only a smile away. I'd probably sell a lot more books and have a lot more people exploring my particular brand of faith. But I'd be lying to say that there is no pain in spiritual growth. I'd be selling you false hope, taking you off the path to happiness and fulfillment, leading you to more pain in the long run. The truth is that spiritual growth involves making choices that go against our lower nature. We choose higher goals, aspirations, achievements that go against our natural grain and tendencies. For instance, if we really want to be spiritual, we need to learn to love other people as much as we love ourselves, to forgive others, to reach out to help others, even those not like ourselves. That's not natural. Our instincts tell us to protect self at all costs, to fight for what we need, to hunt and gather for ourselves lest we be in need, to look out for number one. When we begin to aspire to more noble and loving aims, a battle ensues between two different sets of values. Our higher self battles the lower self. It is a struggle between conflicting wants and needs. I remember hearing a Native American story in which an old man talks of having two wolves battling inside of him, one greedy and one loving. He was asked which one wins in the struggles. He replied, "The one I feed." This is the essence of spiritual growth.

Our instincts to take care of ourselves are not bad, wrong, or evil. They are very useful, God-given, and necessary. The problem arises when our lives default into allowing these instincts to rule us and to be a priority over all other loves, goals, and aspirations. If we place above all other things our desire for self-promotion, material gain, sensual gratification, sexual pleasure, even appetite and personal comfort, these drives become evil. If these are more important to us than loving others, caring for those who need us, respecting other's dignity, rights, possessions, lives, then we are living destructive, evil lives. This selfish way is the old way. The state of rebirth or regeneration occurs when these base loves serve as a foundation for our lives, but the more noble part of us that loves, serves, and honors others is dominant and gives us the greatest value and joy.

The process of growth comes through struggle; our growth is growth that takes place in struggle. For me, these struggles are many and often excruciating, but I make it through them, and I grow. My struggles involve fear and learning to trust in a higher power to care for me. I don't have much trust, and it is hard for me to let go of trying to control most aspects of my life. I struggle to let go of the fear that my family may not have enough to survive or that I will not be able to care for them if I don't work harder and make more money. It is hard for me to trust my children as they grow into adults, that they will make the right choices for their future. I have a hard time letting them go. I constantly remind myself that they are in God's care and that I must trust this. I realize I can't control their fate and that it's harmful to try. I struggle with finding appropriate ways of filling that emptiness inside my heart—the big, black hole —which wants to feel complete, satisfied, and happy. I look for ways of filling that emptiness with spirit, love, the sense of self-worth that comes from serving others, rather than the old ways of quick fixes, thrills, chemicals, and destructive habits. It's often a battle. I find that, as I make progress and it ebbs and flows, I do become happier. I'm more content, inwardly fulfilled, peaceful, sometimes joyful. I can sense that, as I turn from what I consider destructive impulses, I can grow and, through the grace of God, am being reborn each day! That's the process for me. It's sometimes painful, always rewarding, never boring.

When we find ourselves in difficult times of struggle, we may feel that our pain is too much for us or that our difficulties are too great. Sometimes we can feel overwhelmed by fear, grief, rage, guilt, or so many other debilitating emotions that we don't know if we can cope. I often hear people say that we should take heart in times of trouble and misfortune because "God never gives us more than we can handle." I personally believe that this statement is a lie and can cause even more grief, hurt, and shame. With this kind of belief, we might break down in the middle of our pain and struggle, confessing, "I am failing! I am failing God." The truth is that we often get more than we can handle. The key is that what we go through is never more than God can handle. You might say, "God never gives us more that he can handle." We can't do it on our own. We need to learn how to let go and allow a higher power to lead us, the power and love of God. This power is immeasurable, and what it can accomplish is astoundingly beautiful. The result of our struggle and growth is a deep centeredness, a rich life of active love, and a sense of peace that permeates our whole being. Jesus said, "Peace I leave with you; my peace I give to you. I do not give to you as the world gives. Do not let your hearts be troubled, and do not let them be afraid" (John 14:27).

Through persevering in these struggles, we find a deepening understanding and appreciation of what it means to be alive: we become more compassionate, responsible, aware; we become spiritual. In these struggles, we learn that we can't control our own lives or make ourselves better, but that God can. We become willing to let go of our preconceived notions about ourselves and our lives and gain a bigger picture of what life is really like. As we turn from selfishness and desire, we find real happiness and fulfillment in compassion and mutual love for others. As we awaken from a sleepy and obscure focus on meeting natural needs and wants, we discover the exhilarating adventure of spiritual exploration, awareness of higher realities, purposes, and meaning to all things. We awaken to life, to freedom, to our true selves, and to God. This is true rebirth.

Do not be astonished that I said to you, "You must be born again." The wind blows where it chooses, and you hear the sound of it, but you do not know where it comes from or where it goes. So it is with everyone who is born of the Spirit.

John 3:7–8

4

Am I Being Cared For?

Sometime we can feel very alone as we strive to understand the dimensions of this world and our place in it. There are times when we strain to see a force for good working in our lives or in the lives of others. We see much evil and destruction in the world and we wonder why. How can God let such evil things happen? As we are surprised with challenges in our own lives, we may wonder if God is there. We wonder if any of this makes sense. Is there a reason things happen the way they do? Are we being cared for?

God Doesn't Make Bad Things Happen

God doesn't punish people. God doesn't will evil to anyone. God doesn't hurt people. A family lost a child in a terrible accident. Two church leaders came to their door to offer their condolences. They said that they felt great pain for the family, but they also added, "This was God's will" and "We don't always understand why God does what he does, but must accept God's will." What a terrible thing to say! I've heard stories in which this has happened to people, unfortunately more times than I can count. I don't know where this idea came from. I'm sure it didn't come from God. We have already discussed how God is pure love and never wishes harm to anyone. The idea that God wills bad things to happen is not only misguided but potentially devastating. How can someone love a God who wishes them ill or has hurt them? And yet people try to submit to the will of a God that really doesn't offer much in the way of love, mercy, or understanding.

God wills only good for all his people. There is nothing more important to our Creator than for every one of us to have as much happiness and fulfillment as humanly possible. When bad things happen, God feels our pain, is present with us, and works to bring out the best in a bad situation. But we must remember that God takes the long view. His goal is not to give us temporary and perhaps superficial and fleeting comfort in this world, but rather to safeguard our eternal welfare. Remember Jesus' words to Pilate when Pilate asked him if he was a king. He said, "My kingdom is not from this world" (John 18:36). He also said, "Do not worry, saying, 'What will we eat?' or 'What will we drink?'. . . But strive first for the kingdom of God and his righteousness, and all these things will be given to you as well" (Matthew 6:31; 33)

God gave us the opportunity to choose to love and to bring goodness into the world, and as we have seen in chapter one, we are given the opportunity to choose the opposite as well. We can't be free to love if we are not free to hate. We can't be free to show kindness and mercy if we are not free to hurt people, as painful and as contrary to God's love as that may be. People need to be free. When people hurt one another, God takes no delight in it, but he does allow it to happen. When we are affected by the evil of others—for example, by means of criminal acts, terrorism, war, or even when we see others treated poorly by our fellow man—we ask God, "Why?" We can become in-dignant toward him. "If God is so powerful and loving, why doesn't he stop this?" we might say. Within this question lies a hidden doubt that maybe there is no God looking over us or such a weak God that we despise him for his ineptness.

But think about it. Consider what would happen if God stopped the hand of the aggressor every time it was raised. What would happen if God opened up the heavens and shut down the war machines every time nations prepared for battle?

You might think, "That would be great!" But imagine the world waking up that day to the stark reality that we had no real self-determination or choice. What would happen to you if, when you yell at your wife, when you opened your mouth to spout forth your anger, you lost your voice or felt the hand of God covering your mouth, making you unable to speak? Life would become a sham, we would become robots of God, all joy would be taken away from us because we would have lost the most precious gift God has given us—our freedom. God loves us so much that he made us free. Doing evil to others isn't right, but we have the right to do it. Hurting others isn't God's will for the human race, but God has given us free will all the same. Free will is a huge gift from the source of love and life and a huge responsibility to use wisely. The questions we should be asking ourselves are what evil we personally bring into the world and how we can stop it. What can we personally do to help others give up hurting and turn toward mercy instead? What can we do to protect innocent lives and help those who have fallen victim to humanity's abuse of freedom? How can we help God to bring good out of even the worst situation?

God Brings Good out of Everything—If We Let Him

Swedenborg says it is impossible to look God's providence in the face—that is, as it is happening—but we can see it when we reflect on the past. In other words, in times of crisis, it is hard to sense that God is present and working to bring good out of a bad situation. However, when we look back at such times, we can often see the gentle hand of God at work. I know that I have often experienced this upon reflection. I can see times when I was disappointed by the direction my life seemed to be turning toward but later realized that this turn was exactly what I needed. I have seen times of sorrow in my life bring a deeper sense of spiritual connection to God and the reality of life after death and heaven. One of the worst times in my life, involving an untimely death, gave me an opportunity to be a helper and a guardian angel to two of my dear friends, a treasured relationship that lasts to this day. I would never desire tragedy as a means of growth, even as we pray in the Lord's Prayer, "Lead us not into temptation;" but I am amazed and dumbfounded at the good God manages to bring out of even the worst evil. Look at the horrible act of terrorism of September 11, 2001, something so far from God's will and even more horrible to be committed in God's name. However, the love and charity that poured out of all people, not only in the United States, but throughout the world, was astounding! Cynics say that this was temporary and fleeting, but didn't a part of us change forever? Or, at the very least, did we not have that opportunity presented before us in this horrific time in our lives? God didn't make this event happen or will it, but God didn't abandon us. God was there in an extremely important way, working through the same human freedom and choice he gave those terrorists, but now the choice of thousands was love and compassion and a resolve to rid the world of such hideous crimes.

In times of tragedy, we may not be able to see immediately that God is there, leading us to peace, comfort, and so much more. However, we can rest assured that this world has been set up in such a way that all can be bent and turned toward good. God provides constantly that the choice for good is always present and continually lifts us up from our pain and doubt to freedom to live and love again. The real question is whether we trust this. Can we find the good, or at least pursue it, and allow the force of love and life to lift us up? When we do this, we can heal and even grow. And this growth is eternal.

The sole purpose of our creation is that we may be prepared for a life of happiness and eternal growth in heaven. This world is like the preparation period in the womb, where we are formed into the kind of people we will be for eternity. The difference from a child's being formed in the womb and our being formed in this world for heaven is that we make the choice as to how we will be formed. God gives us the choice to love, to give, to grow. When we see people suffer, we wonder how God can let that happen. When someone we love is tragically taken away from us, we grieve for that person, for all the times and experiences in this world he or she will miss. This is important. Grieving for others is an act of love. But it is also important to take the long view. If life in this world is only a preparation for a life in heaven, even when someone is taken early from this world, God's dream for that person comes true. Those who have left this world are with God forever in heaven. Also, life in this world is but a blink of the eye compared to the eternity of heaven. Suffering hurts, and no one can say that it is intrinsically a good thing; but it is so temporal, temporary, and fleeting compared to heaven that you can think of the worst situation on earth as being the prick of a pin compared to the decades, centuries, ten thousand light years and beyond of peace, contentment, joy, and growth.

When we go through hard times, we don't have to like it. God doesn't like us to suffer, and we don't have to like it either. It's wrong, and it hurts. But we can make it even worse by our attitude. When we focus on this world alone, we fear death, we run from suffering, we yearn for moments of pleasure and bodily comfort. All of these are part of the enjoyment of this world. But this isn't all there is. This is just the beginning. Through all of life's experiences, we can learn and grow; and although God doesn't will evil or cause it, he does ensure that we can learn and grow through all of our experiences here in this moment of preparation. It is important to remember the psalmist's words, "Weeping may linger for the night, but joy comes with the morning" (Psalm 30:5), and this "morning" is eternal.

Jesus said, "Consider the lilies, how they grow: they neither toil nor spin; yet I tell you, even Solomon in all his glory was not clothed like one of these. But if God so clothes the grass of the field, which is alive today and tomorrow is thrown into the oven, how much more will he clothe you—you of little faith?" (Luke 12:27–28) God is continually caring for each of us, seeing that his dream for us comes true—that we may be with him in heaven. The choice is ours, and we can make that choice every moment of the day. There is a passage from Swedenborg's book *Arcana Coelestia* §8478:2–4 that I find profound. It begins by stating,

> People are concerned about the morrow when they are not content with their lot, do not trust in God but in themselves, and have solely worldly and earthly things in view, and not heavenly ones. These people are ruled completely by anxiety over the future, and by the desire to possess all things and exercise control over all people. That desire is kindled and grows greater and greater, till at length it is beyond all measure. They grieve if they do not realize the objects of their desires, and they are distressed at the loss of them. Nor can they find any consolation, for in times of loss they are angry with the Divine. They reject him together with all belief, and curse themselves.

I can relate to this. This is hell. When I am in this kind of state, I feel as if I'm in hell because I can't get over my fear and my desire to control my world and others, can't feel satisfied that I am being cared for and have enough, and grieve because of my losses and also of potential losses, realizing I'm never going to be rich or famous, or own that dream house or car, or see the world at my leisure, and on and on. I know many people feel this way when they focus on externals or worldly concerns. Isn't it hell when you feel this way? It ultimately ends in being angry at God for not giving us what we want. We don't recognize the blessings we are given, especially the spiritual opportunities, connections, and gifts, but rather mourn what we do not have.

The passage from *Arcana Coelestia* continues:

> Those who trust in the Divine are altogether different. Though concerned about the morrow, yet they are unconcerned, in that they are not anxious, let alone worried, when they give thought to the morrow. They remain even-tempered whether or not they realize their desires, and they do not grieve over loss; they are content with their lot. If they become wealthy they do not become infatuated with wealth; if they are promoted to important positions they do not consider themselves worthier than others. If they become poor they are not made miserable either; if lowly in status they do not feel downcast. They know that for those who trust in the Divine all things are moving towards an everlasting state of happiness, and that no matter what happens at any time to them, it contributes to that state.

Wow! I can't claim to be in this spiritual state. In fact, when I first read this passage, I was expecting Swedenborg to end by saying, "And these people are called 'saints'." But we are these people, just as we are also the other people who don't trust in the Divine. We can let go of fear and control. We can learn to trust. We can change our attitude toward life so that we allow God to bring good into every situation. The key is to trust that God's providence and creation are moving us towards "an everlasting state of happiness," and this is true no matter what happens. I see this as the crux of what it means to have faith in God. Faith involves knowing that God can save and lift us up, no matter how far we have fallen, no matter how hurt we have become, no matter what circumstance we may be in, if—and this is the key—if we are willing to be lifted up.

Swedenborg's passage concludes by explaining that we can go with the flow of providence, very similar to the philosophy of Taoism and the Way, although Swedenborg was unfamiliar with Lao Tzu's teachings:

> It should be recognized that Divine providence is over-all, that is, it is present within the smallest details of all, and that people in the stream of providence are being carried along constantly towards happier things, whatever appearance that means may present. Those in the stream of providence are people who trust in the Divine and ascribe everything to Him. . . . It should also be recognized that to the extent that anyone is in the stream of providence she/he is in a state of peace; and the extent that anyone is in a state of peace by virtue of the good of faith, the person is in the Divine providence. These alone know and believe that the Lord's Divine providence resides within every single thing, indeed within the smallest details of all, as well as that the Divine providence has what is eternal in view.

There is an invisible and gentle current in each one of our lives that can peacefully carry us to happiness and heaven. It is always there for us, whenever we want to let go and trust the way. Even in what might appear as the worst of times, that stream is flowing and can carry us to all things blessed. We can trust that we are being cared for, that our eternal happiness is the most important thing God has in mind for us, and that all of crea-tion flows toward this end. Our choice is to believe this, accept it, and freely choose it. Let go and let God. Wade into the stream. Relax, and enjoy the ride.

5

What Is The Bible Telling Us?

How do we learn about things like heaven, God, the spiritual life? We all experience intuitions about what God or heaven might be like or have some perception about how to live spiritually. But, for the most part, we need to learn these things from an outside source. Books on spirituality, written revelations from the great world religions, even other people's opinions about these spiritual subjects can help us gain a view about life that we simply can't gain on our own. Learning from others, especially from what God has told us in revelation, gives us a higher perspective, a way of looking at life from God's point of view rather than our own. Turning to a higher source for knowledge helps us move out of our limited and often closed worldview to a new, aware, and growing understanding of all things.

The world is full of wisdom, knowledge, and an abundance of advice about how we should live our lives. Much of this information is very helpful. Anyone who is serious about spiritual growth will be reading a lot of material about it, sifting through to what seems to ring true and what might be incorporated into their own life and belief system. For my own spiritual path, as well as in preparation for writing several books on spirituality, I have experienced an amazing adventure in exploring all the major religions and their views about what it means to live with love and integrity. I have grown to love, for instance, the Tao Te Ching, as well as the Dhammapada (the sayings of Buddha); and I also love exploring Native American spirituality, as well as anything on the variety of spiritual rituals and traditions of varying religious cultures. Studying these other approaches helped me to understand and appreciate the variety of spiritual paths and sacred traditions.

The first course of action I recommend to people who come to me to gain a stronger connection to spirituality is to start reading spiritual literature, especially the various revelations found in the major religions of the world because these can help the person build a foundation of belief. They offer choices of belief and many insights, techniques, and sacred ways of living that will enrich any seeker's spiritual life.

I also fully recommend reading the teachings of Emanuel Swedenborg because I have never found any teachings so invigorating, freeing, and ringing as true as I have in these works. Indeed, the very premise of Swedenborg's teachings is that there is good in all religions and that we should never stop looking for truth. I like that foundational view, rather than one that tells me I should stop looking and just believe what I am told. I believe Swedenborg's books are the foundation for not only a new life but for a new spiritual era for humanity.

There is a book, however, that is written so differently and is so profoundly powerful because of how it is written that it is unlike any other book in the world. It is designed in such a way that it contains levels upon levels of spiritual meaning, so that, when one reads this book in humility looking for answers, answers are given that are not present on the literal page. This book is a window to heaven, a constant connection to God, and a guide for life. It is God speaking to us. In fact, it's called the Word of God. Yes, I'm talking about what most people refer to as the Bible. Swedenborg calls this book the "Crown of all Revelations" in *True Christianity* §11, and I have to agree. I can only speak for myself, but I have found over years of study that this book is rich with meaning. The treasures inside the Bible are immeasurable. I have found a nugget here and a gem there in other spiritual writings and revelations, but the Bible is like an endless mine of fine gems of all kind, streams of gold and silver, and endless and boundless potential for beauty in the wisdom and love offered within those pages. I believe if you can approach the Bible from a different point of view than, perhaps, the one you grew up with, you can find these treasures too.

A Metaphor about Our Relationship with God

First of all, if you feel you have been burned or turned off by that literalistic, judgmental view of the Bible, don't worry. What I am going to tell you is nothing like that. People who claim they "take the Bible completely literally" and then go on to tell you how wrong you are and how you need to be saved as they are, and so on and so forth, may have a lot of passion for what they believe but they are mistaken. No one can take the Bible completely literally, and they shouldn't. Jesus says, "If your right eye causes you to sin, tear it out and throw it away" (Matthew 5:29). Don't do it! God encourages his people to dash their enemy's infants against the rocks (Psalm 137:8). Don't even think God means it! God says he creates evil as well as good (Isaiah 45:7). Don't believe it! In the biblical story of Creation, God created light on the first day but didn't create the sun until the fourth day. The disciples were promised they would see the second coming of Christ before they passed away from earthly life. It didn't happen.

Contradictions exist all through the Bible, and one cannot take it completely literally or live by everything God commands within it. The reason is that this holy book is to be explored deeper to see the underlying meanings, the real heart of what is being said, the spiritual story behind the historical story. The Word of God is a metaphor, a mirror in which we behold ourselves, a series of parables that beg us to look deeper and welcome us to a world of pictures, symbols, and the soul of spirituality clothed in rich storytelling.

What can be taken literally in the Bible is fairly clear. The plain statements that ring true in every religion, the basic laws of morality, love and charity, to live with spirit and integrity, to resist evil, to pursue goodness, to follow the higher path—these teachings and more can easily be adopted as eternal verities. The historical aspects of the Bible, the history of the Israelites, of the prophets and kings, of Jesus himself can be taken literally, if one chooses. There was a Moses. The Israelites did leave Egypt and settle in Canaan. A series of judges, kings, and prophets did rise up. I believe that even the miracles happened, one way or another.

But many things said have a deeper meaning, and the history itself is a metaphor for our own lives. For instance, when we are told to pluck out our right eye, that right eye symbolizes a way of seeing the world that we must remove from our being if we are to be whole. The enemy's children God says are to be destroyed are the spiritual enemies of our own predisposition to anger, resentment, lust, hatred, the offspring of which we know all too well—acts of selfishness and cruelty. These must be destroyed if we wish to escape the tyranny of our own destructive nature. The story of Creation is a parable of each one of us being created anew. The light created on the first day is the first dawn of spiritual consciousness in each of us, when we "see the light" and know that there is such a thing as truth. Light is the symbol of truth. The births of the sun and moon on the fourth day are symbolic of the birth of love and faith in our lives. The Second Coming is a coming in spirit and in a new understanding of God. These things must be seen for their deeper meaning.

Joseph Campbell, the author of the *Power of Myth* and many books on symbolism in ancient cultures, says that all the old mythologies were stories that held special meaning for their people. These stories reflected deeper lessons for people to learn about life, about themselves, about spirit and about the Divine. They may have been taken literally by some, but most also knew the deeper symbolism. Campbell also said many times in his lectures that the problem with our Western world is that we've become so scientific and externally focused that we have rejected mythology as meaningless. We have no stories that we hold dear to reflect our lives and all that surrounds us.

What Swedenborg indicated in his works, well before Campbell was even born, is that the Bible is that story. The Bible is the sacred mythology, so to speak, of the Judeo-Christian culture. It is story of our lives, our God, our spiritual heritage on a deeper level, our destiny as a people. This is why, after the resurrection, "beginning with Moses and all the prophets, [Jesus] interpreted to them the things about himself in all the scriptures" (Luke 24:27), and also "Jesus told the crowds all these things in parables; without a parable he told them nothing" (Matthew 13:34). Instead of locking into a literal interpretation of this book and limiting its wisdom to one level of meaning, when we see that it is a parable with level upon level of rich meaning, the Bible opens up to us like a window into eternity and light shines through it from heaven. The wisdom becomes never-ending. The beauty ever deepens. The depth of meaning grows and grows. Our connection to God through this book strengthens. We begin to understand why the Bible is called God's Word—not simply because someone said so or even simply because its literal meaning often refers to God, but because we see and sense God in every story, in every parable, in every saying, in every symbolic meaning. This is why it is the crown of revelations.

The Key to Unlocking the Bible's Meaning

Swedenborg says that all of creation is a mirror in which we can behold the face of God. In ancient times, people close to the earth were well aware of the deep symbolism in all that they saw around them. They knew that different animals represented various archetypical reflections of their own states of being. In Native American religion and some African religions, these were called totems or spirit animals. But in the most ancient times, even the sun, moon, and stars had spiritual significance, as well as all parts of creation, such as earth, wind, fire, water, and everything in between. This knowledge, or rather the inner perception of the spiritual significance of all things, was the heart and soul of the most ancient forms of religion found in indigenous cultures around the world. What happened through the process of time is that, as people became less spirit-focused, they lost sight of the spiritual significance in the world around them. For some, instead of seeing the face of God in nature, they saw nature as God. For some, who had developed statues and icons representing the various aspects of God, as they lost their spiritual roots, they began to worship the statues and icons themselves as gods.

At the same time that people were losing their perceptive ability to see the world of spirit reflected in the world of nature, a new type of symbolic language was appearing, that of the written word. Swedenborg says that this spiritual symbolism began to show up in ancient writing and storytelling. Every aspect of these stories reflected spiritual truths that explained something about God or about humanity or even about life in general. The mythologies of ancient explorers reflected human exploration of the mysteries of the world. The stories of heroes battling monsters reflected people's inward battles against their own personal demons, such as fear, hatred, and want. The ancient stories of creation and the great flood, both of which can be found in the Bible, are stories that show up on different continents in many ancient mythologies and writings. They are stories reflective of the spiritual state of humanity in ancient days. Creation is symbolic of each individual's being created anew, and the flood signifies how turning away from the order of life and love that God has created for us inundates us with fallacies that suffocate our spirituality.

Tradition says that the first stories in the book of Genesis were collected from ancient times by Moses as he put together the first five books of the Old Testament, commonly called the Pentateuch. They were seen as parables containing deeper truths. As the Old Testament was added to over time, the historical accounts themselves were also symbolic of spiritual realities. Thus the story of the Israelites escaping from Egypt, struggling through the wilderness, and eventually securing the Promised Land is a parable of each person's struggles to escape his or her own inner slavery to selfishness, fear, and want, the struggle through times of doubt and temptation, and the eventual procuring of a happy and heavenly way of life. But all of the stories, whether of the prophets or the kings, or even the events contained within the Gospels and the book of Revelation, contain these deeper meanings hidden in symbols. When the symbolism is known, the stories come alive and give power to the deeper spiritual truths within them. Because these deeper truths about life are couched in story, they have power, stick with us, and contain deeper meaning through metaphor.

This is what makes the Bible special. It contains layer after layer of spiritual meaning within the literal stories themselves. The potential discovery of the truths within this book is literally limitless.

Every story has deeper meanings within it. And every aspect of that story is symbolic. For instance, when Jesus spoke to the Samaritan woman at the well, he told her that he could give her "living water" (John 4:11), and the proclamation is given at the end of the book of Revelation that all may now, "take of the water of life as a gift" (Rev. 22:17). Water, when used in a positive sense, is symbolic of cleansing or healing truth. Jesus says whoever drinks of his water will never thirst (John 4:14). We see this in the story of Naaman's being cleansed of his leprosy when he washes in the River Jordan. Leprosy is symbolic of spiritual numbness and atrophy that come from, to use modern terms, living in your head rather than your heart. John baptized people in the name of the Messiah to come as a symbol of people preparing themselves to receive the truth that would soon be revealed by Jesus. He said, "I baptize you with water; but one who is more powerful than I is coming; I am not worthy to untie the thong of his sandals. He will bap-tize you with the Holy Spirit and fire" (Luke 3:16). The Holy Spirit is Jesus' spirit, and the fire is a symbol of love. This is why Jesus also said, "I came to bring fire to the earth, and how I wish it were already kindled" (Luke 12:49). Both fire and water rep-resent love and truth; but when used in the negative sense, they become the opposite. The raging fires that destroy are symbolic of hatred and burning lust that consume a person's insides. The damaging floods in both the Bible and in creation itself sym-bolize a flood of false persuasion that can suffocate our inner life and carry us away beyond our power.

Every word in the Bible has spiritual meaning or several deeper meanings when read in context. Let me give you an example from the first and most commonly shared tale among all cultures, the story of creation. As I said earlier, the creation story is a parable that illustrates how each human can be created anew by God. In the beginning, there is darkness and void. This is our state before the dawn of even the consciousness of spirituality. We live in darkness and feel the emptiness of a purposeless life. God says, "Let there be light," and light illuminates the first of creation. This is the first dawn of spiritual consciousness. As is often said in common language, we begin to "see the light" or the reality of our situation. The light separated from the darkness and the firmament separating the waters above from the waters below are both symbolic of the dawning awareness within us that there is such a thing as truth and such a thing as fallacy. We recognize that there are higher, more spiritual truths or realities, represented by the waters above, and lower realities or factual truths represented by the waters below. The dry land appearing between these waters is our conscious mind, which will bring forth much growth. The herbs, grass, and fruit trees that begin to grow upon the earth symbolize the sprouting of our first loving actions. Our life is beginning to blossom gently like the tender shoot of new spring-like growth. As I said earlier, the sun, moon, and stars are the birth of love, faith, and an abundance of insights that await us as we grow. The fish symbolize great schools of knowledge that flourish within the sea of our unconscious minds. The birds symbolize all sorts of beautiful thoughts that can soar into the heavens and bask in the light of the sun. The animals symbolize all the new feelings and what Swedenborg calls "affections" for what is good, loving, and true. The dignity of the lion, the innocence of the lamb, the playfulness of a chipmunk, the steadfastness of an ox, and every other sense of being are born within us. The creation of the first man is symbolic of the creation of each one of us anew, in the image and likeness of our Creator. Having been given rule over all creation is not, as some have suggested, divine permission to dominate all creatures of the earth, but rather to rule over everything within one's self. It is symbolic of what is often called in Eastern spirituality "self-mastery," yet through the loving power of the divine guiding within. And so, we are told that God saw everything that he had created and that "indeed, it was very good," (Genesis 1:31). God's resting on the seventh day is symbolic of his work finding completion within our very beings and his divine love and wisdom finding a resting place within us. "He will dwell with them; they will be his peoples and God himself will be with them" (Revelation 21: 3).

Let's examine the deeper meaning of the story of the Exodus.[1] The children of Israel found themselves slaves in Egypt under a megalomaniac pharaoh, which is symbolic of our own servitude to our egos and destructive behavior. The plagues that fall upon Egypt symbolize the spiritual calamities we bring upon ourselves when we, like pharaoh, stubbornly refuse to let go and allow change in our lives. Each plague has a specific meaning. Locusts and flies represent the type of deranged thinking that can take over and uncontrollably buzz in our heads. The sickness of the cattle symbolizes the ill feelings we develop: fear, want, insecurity, doubt. The darkness sym-bolizes our own spiritual darkness. Finally, like an addict of any kind, we can hit bottom. Pharaoh loses his first-born child, as do all of the Egyptians. As a result, he lets the children of Israel go. When we've lost it all or see that we could lose everything important to us, for the first time we are ready to let go and let God lead us. Moses, who is symbolic of God's law that leads us, takes us away from all this suffering.

The children of Israel wander in the wilderness for forty years. The number forty is symbolic of spiritual trial and temp-tation. Everywhere that number is used in the Bible we find some sort of turmoil going on. Life is a journey, a time of uncer-tainty, hunger and thirst, and full of many trials. The Israelites' being fed manna in the wilderness and drinking water from rocks symbolize God's care, even in times when we don't feel connected to him. Manna symbolizes the inner sense of spiritual peace and connection to God that we feel from

---

1. For a more detailed explanation of how the Exodus story can be applied to a spiritual recovery program, see my work *Return to the Promised Land* (West Chester, Pa.: Chrysalis Books, 1998).

time to time on our journey. It is not very perceptible in the beginning. Manna means literally "what is it?" It is not recognized as being very significant, but it does serve. These inner feelings of spirit and life are enough to sustain us until we reach the "milk and honey" joy of a new spiritual life represented by the Promised Land. The water that sustains the wanderers on their journey, as said earlier, symbolizes the living truth that sustains us. When thirsty, we are given assurances deep within that we can get by, that there is a purpose, that we will grow. Much of the time as we search for truth we do thirst, but we are given what we need, until the time when water flows freely in our new spiritual life.

Israel's fighting for and conquering the Promised Land is symbolic of the battles we face against our own destructive tendencies that are encamped within us and must be removed, with God's help, before we can have peace. Each enemy symbolizes a certain type of evil or dysfunction. Each city symbolizes a powerful spiritual force that blocks our progress. For instance, Jericho represents a well-fortified but destructive way of being within us. The wall around the enemy is the false ideas and excuses we tell ourselves to protect that way of being. It could be selfishness, self-pity, resentment, or laziness. You probably know what the Jericho inside of you is. Blowing the trumpets at those walls is telling yourself the truth, allowing the truth about your life and those lies to sound out and force those walls of denial to crumble. Once the walls crumble, the destructive nature hidden within is exposed and can be conquered.

The taking of the Promised Land is symbolic of entering a new spiritual way of living and being. Peace comes to our minds and hearts. The fruits around us are the beautiful experiences of life that sustain us as we grow into spiritual beings. The milk and honey of the Promised Land symbolize spiritual happiness and even delight. This story, like the story of Creation, is about how we are made spiritual and new.

Imagine, with the key to understanding the deeper meaning of the Bible, how much more all the stories within could mean to each of us. They come alive. They make sense. They relate directly to our lives.[2] As Swedenborg wrote in *Doctrine of Holy Scripture* §3, "The Word [Bible] is such that there is holiness in every sentence, and in every word, and in some places in even the very letters. This is why the Word conjoins man with the Lord, and opens heaven."

---

2. Swedenborg's works give us the keys we need to unlocking these stories. I encourage you to pursue knowledge of this inner meaning in his work *Arcana Coelestia.*

6

Does Love Last Forever?

The love that a man and woman share in marriage can be one of the greatest gifts from God to humankind. In his book *Marital Love*, Swedenborg describes this married love as having a divine origin. It comes from and reflects the divine marriage of love and wisdom in God and is also the provenance of the human race itself. This is why the Bible says in the very first chapter of Genesis, "So God created humankind in his image, in the image of God he created them; male and female he created them" (Genesis 1:27). Because of the origin and use of marriage, the love in marriage has more potential than any other. In *Marital Love* §57, Swedenborg writes, "Regarded from its origin and correspondence, this love is celestial, spiritual, holy, pure and clean, more so than any other love which exists from the Lord in angels of heaven or people of the earth. It is the fundamental love of all celestial, spiritual, and consequently natural loves. Moreover into this love have been gathered all joys and delights from the first to the last of them." This ideal love, often called "conjugial love" in the New Church, is not necessarily confined to what we typically think of as romantic love but is something much deeper, more spiritual and enduring. Love in marriage is a deep friendship, a loving commitment to one partner, a tender relationship built from years of life and growth together.

Those who are in love know it. Poets write about it. Hollywood makes movies about it. But rarely do we find a church that teaches that true love never dies. It doesn't end in death, as repeated in so many marriage ceremonies, "Until death do you part." True love is everlasting. It cannot die. Those who truly love each other will dwell together in heaven after death. Their love and their care for each other remain and even grow. Their joy in working together in service to God and to other fellow human beings flourishes in the afterlife, and their love takes on a newness each day.

When a couple approaches their marriage with the belief that their love is eternal, it raises up the marriage to a new dimension from simply an earthly, temporal contract to something spiritual, above time and space. The commitments and the promises that they make to each other are on the level of soulmates, forever blessed with the other's love and companionship, a condition that perfects them. How contrary to this is the traditional view of marriage, especially held by those religious sects who place women and men on unequal footing. This is the reason that, when Jesus was asked by the Sadducees if a woman had seven husbands in this life whom she would end up with in heaven, he replied, "In the resurrection they neither marry nor are given in marriage" (Matthew 22:30). The kind of contract the Sadducees envisioned when they thought of marriage, as was typical of the time, was that women were possessions, and marriage was a legal bond and no more. That kind of marriage doesn't exist in heaven. Both partners are different but equal. Both come to the relationship in freedom, with an inner commitment and love. Therefore, Swedenborg writes, "When married partners love each other tenderly, they think of eternity in regard to the marriage covenant, and not at all of it ending with death" (*Marital Love* §206). For those who genuinely love each other, their love never dies; their relationship grows forever.

Spiritual Growth and Marriage

The core of any growing relationship is a strong commitment to God. The New Church believes strongly in a loving, divinely human concept of God, who has revealed himself to humankind as the Lord Jesus Christ. Marriages based on a strong belief in the Lord and his teachings flourish because he is the source of all that is good and true, and he alone has the power to help the couple overcome the many obstacles to a loving relationship. Genuine marriage is not a state of infatuation, where two look to each other for their only fulfillment, but rather a mutual looking above self to a Greater Power for help and guidance and as a source of fulfillment.

The Lord, in his essence, is pure love. He does not condemn, does not desire to fill us with guilt or shame, is not an angry father who desires to punish his children for their sins. As we have seen, this view of God is hurtful in general, but it is particularly hurtful to a marriage, for it alienates a couple from the love that God has to offer and the help that he can bring to the man and woman who have vowed to live their lives as one. If a couple brings this living, reachable, and divinely human God into their relationship, they have someone real and all-powerful to rely upon: the Lord himself.

With a couple's commitment to the Lord, it makes sense that spiritual life and marriage work together hand in hand. To the degree that a couple uses the basic principles of genuine Christianity in their marriage, they will be blessed in their marital relationship. The Lord has taught us much about forgiveness and faithfully fulfilling our duties and our promises. When we apply these same teachings to marriage, we set a course toward happier lives. There is no better opportunity to become a spiritual person than in learning to live, work, and play together with a life-partner. It is often said that charity begins in the home; and when we learn the art of love with our spouse, we are in turn blessed with a rich and meaningful companionship. The Lord has said, "Give and it will be given unto you." This is true in marriage as in any other relationship.

Marriages have their challenges. If a couple believes they will get by on love alone, they may be in for some rough realizations. Love needs to be clothed in truth. The teachings of the God's Word are that clothing. They give a person structure for that love, and like clothing, they protect the love from harm. For instance, many marriages are challenged by times of temptation, whether these temptations entail sexual allurement, power struggles, or conflict of values. Turning away from selfishness and lust guards against the destructive forces that would harm our love relationships. People make mistakes, and all couples experience their ups and downs in marriage; but when religion and marriage walk hand in hand, the means for continued development remain at hand.

In fact, when a person looks to God as a power greater than self, prays for help, and shuns selfish thoughts and desires as sins against God, he or she will find happiness in all relationships and aspects of life. Jesus said, "The kingdom of God is within you" (Luke 17:21). We create our own state of heaven or hell right now, while we are on earth, and this state follows us after death and comes into its fullness. Thus married couples who use the tools for spiritual growth given to us in the Bible, as well as in the teachings of the New Church, create within themselves and within their relationship a heavenly state and way of life.

The Lord Provides

Swedenborg also wrote that those who do not find a life-partner in this world can and will find an eternal partner in afterlife, if they so desire and if they prepare themselves for such a heavenly union. People prepare themselves for this love by becoming willing to follow God and by turning away from what is selfish and hurtful, learning to love what is good and true. All are prepared for this love when they turn away from lust and especially adultery, which is opposite to the love of marriage. Swedenborg writes in *Marital Love* §49 that those who, "from youth have loved, chosen, and asked of the Lord a legitimate and lovely partnership with one, and who spurn and reject wandering lusts as an offense to their nostrils," will find such a partner, if not in this world, then in the life to come.

Swedenborg teaches that those who trust in the Lord are gently led by his stream of providence. "They are all the time carried along toward everything that is happy, whatever may be the appearance of the means; and those are in the stream of Providence who put their trust in the Divine and attribute all things to him," he states in *Arcana Coelestia* §8478. Whether we are single or married, the Lord is leading us to the greatest potential for good in our lives. We can, of course, swim against this gentle current, but those who trust in the Lord and allow him to guide them are carried toward heaven and heavenly happiness.

Most marriages today have very little foundation in God and are not based on spiritual principles. Marriages today are for the most part earthly contracts that are sadly all too often broken. The Lord knows that marriage can be hard work and that relationships fail. He asks us to do the best we can. When Jesus said that the only cause for divorce is adultery, his disciples responded that perhaps it was better, then, not to marry at all. Jesus replied, "Not everyone can accept this teaching, but only those to whom it is given. . . . Let anyone accept this who can" (Matthew 19:11–13). This sounds to me as if Jesus is presenting us with an ideal and telling us to do the best we can. In modern terms, I hear him saying, "Look, marriage is tough. But this is the way it is. Strive for it, if you can."

And so what Swedenborg puts forth for a new Christianity is a new vision of marriage and new hope for lasting love in marriage. It is a dream to believe in and an ideal to strive for. Couples who approach the Lord with a sincere heart and rely on the Lord and his teachings as their guide and source of life and love will be carried within that stream toward all things blessed, happy, and delightful—forever.

Once when I was pastor of a congregation that met in a cafe in Rogers Park, Chicago, many single people came to see what we had to offer in such a unique place as this setting. Some of these young people came out of lives of incredible pain, as they searched for love in, as they say, all the wrong places and found humiliation, emptiness, and shame instead. I remember preaching the ideals of marriage and the love for one partner and how a promiscuous life was actually selfish, unhappy, and hurtful. I wondered if what I said would be accepted. I was surprised to find out that practically everyone there nodded in affirmation throughout my sermon. I asked why afterward. I was told again and again, "I know what you are saying is true because I've been down that lonely road." At the same time, I witnessed the same young people notice each other, fall in love, and embrace the new ideals of marriage they were hearing. I was deeply moved to be a part of that renewal in their lives.

I will never forget one particular bride and want to share with you her words to me in the center aisle of the sanctuary just before her wedding. I was putting on my robe in the vestry next to the sanctuary, preparing for a wedding of a wonderful couple who had each come from a difficult and "out there" life as a single person. They had been with the New Church for two years and met and fell in love with each other at the church. As I finished putting on my robe, I heard someone crying in the sanctuary. I opened the door and peered out to see the bride, halfway up the aisle sobbing. I immediately thought something must be terribly wrong. Perhaps the groom had left or there was some accident. I hurried to her, put my hand on her shoulder, and asked what was wrong. She looked up at me and then back down to the floor and blurted out, "I'm not worthy. I'm not worthy." When I asked what she meant, she said, "After all I've done and been through, I never dreamed I'd find not only the hope for marriage I found in this church, but also my husband to live and grow with forever. I am so happy that God gave them to me. I'm not worthy."

Her tears were tears of joy. I must confess that I found it hard not to tear up myself when officiating at their ceremony twenty minutes later and still tend to tear up when I think of her humble gratitude to this day. And yes, they are still married and have a bunch of kids.

7

Is There An Afterlife?

We will never die. Certainly our bodies will die, but we are more than a body. We are spirit and life from God, created to live forever. Jesus said, "In my Father's house there are many dwelling places. If it were not so, would I have told you that I go to prepare a place for you?" (John 14:2). We are all created for a unique place in heaven, just as Jesus said to the thief on the cross: "Truly I tell you, today you will be with me in Paradise" (Luke 23:43).

When someone we love dies, even those who have lived a full life in this world and pass away in old age, we grieve for their loss. We cherish our memories and honor the good they did in the world. For some who find it difficult to believe in the afterlife, the experience of another's death can be a very sad time because they feel that the departed has dissipated out of existence, never to be seen again. But this doesn't make sense. Since we were created by an eternal God, we can sense deep within ourselves that we will never die. Many people instinctively know that there is life after death, not because they desire it to be so but because deep within, at the core of their being, they sense it. I know that I have little doubt about the reality of the afterlife. I feel it. I sense it. I have experienced so many glimpses of it or have been miraculously touched by it that I cannot doubt. I can have some question as to where I might end up, but I do not question that the other world is real. Perhaps you have that sense, too. Swedenborg put it this way in *Arcana Coelestia* §68, "I have seen, I have heard, I have felt."

A lot of people have seen, heard, and felt. Studies have been done on countless individuals all over the world who have had a near-death experience. It has been estimated that millions have had some sort of contact with an afterlife when close to death themselves. Skeptics may call this experience wishful thinking. But people of all faiths, even those of no faith, both young and old, of every culture and background have reported the same things again and again. They wake up in another dimension happy, healthy, and whole. They see relatives and friends. They experience a beautiful light. Those who have been clinically dead for a longer time see cities of light, beautiful countryside, and angels. What is very interesting is that most of what is reported by those who have had the near-death experience was also reported by Emanuel Swedenborg of his experiences some two hundred years before researchers began recording such a phenomenon. But this experience is also reflected in the Bible, as Jesus assures us that we live on. "And as for the resurrection of the dead, have you not read what was said to you by God, 'I am the God of Abraham, the God of Isaac, and the God of Jacob'? He is God not of the dead, but of the living" (Matthew 22:31–32).

I am most familiar with what Swedenborg said about his journeys to the other side of life. His remarkable experiences lasted the final twenty-seven years of his life, and he wrote of his otherworldly travels in many works, the most famous of which is *Heaven and Hell*. Below are some of his extraordinary findings, related to him by angels. What he learned is that our final journey begins with the choices we make on this earth.

Each of Us Was Born to Be an Angel

This world is a preparation period for eternal life to come. Here we choose what and who we will become. We choose what we will love, how we will reflect that love in life, what we will contribute to this universe and beyond, forever. Just imagine! When God created us and breathed into us the breath of life, what wonderful dreams he had—and still has—for each of us. We were created by the source of love itself as a gift to the rest of humanity from the day of our birth and forevermore.

In *Divine Providence* §27 Swedenborg writes, "Divine Love . . . has the goal of a heaven made up of people who have become and are becoming angels, people with whom it can share all the bliss and joy of love and wisdom, giving them these blessings from the Lord's own presence with them." The word *angel* means "messenger" in the original language in the Bible. We can all be angels, messengers of love and wisdom, truth, mercy, and spirit. Angels are not, as many assume, beings created in another dimension or some sort of super-spiritual human race. (This is the same with devils, or evil spirits, who were all once people too.) Heaven consists of human beings who once walked the earth and used that preparation period on earth to learn to live and grow in the image and likeness of their Creator. Once in heaven, they become free of evil and dysfunction and join a path of eternal growth and happiness. Each one of us is called to this path. We are called to become those messengers of love. We can turn away from what is selfish, or even hellish, in our lives, seek after the truth, live by it, love by it, and allow heaven to flow into us and through us. We can become vessels of the Divine, angels of God.

If, in this life, we have chosen to act as angels, then in the next life, we will be admitted into an angelic society. Angels are powerful beings. Because they have learned to live in and from the Divine, they are able to tap into that divine power, especially against anything evil and false. Just as someone in our world who is very connected to what is right and true will have much personal power over destructive allurements or delusions, the angels see right through deception and spurious arguments. In *Heaven and Hell* §229, Swedenborg states "I have seen angels scatter some hundreds of thousands of evil spirits and cast them into hell. A vast multitude is powerless against them. The skills and wiles and alliances of evil spirits amount to nothing. Angels see everything and dispel it instantly."

Since angels are human beings who once lived in this world, this means we can have that power too. Becoming one with the Divine gives us this power against any fallacious and destructive influence from hell. Real spiritual power is based in and from the source of life power. When we tap into that source, we tap into that power for good.

The Kingdom of God Is within You

Heaven and hell are real places, but they are places of the spirit. The spirit starts right here inside of us. We create our own heaven and hell while we are in this world. When we form a life of love for God and our fellow human beings, we create a heavenly way of life for ourselves right here on earth. We become heavenly beings. As Swedenborg wrote in *Heaven and Hell* §408, "heaven consists in a heartfelt desire for the good of others rather than our own good. It is serving others from love to promote their happiness, not for the sake of any selfish hope of reward."

We can also create hell in our lives. When we are self-centered and act in a hellish manner, we bring the pain and suffering of evil into our own lives. This is easy to see with some who have trashed their lives with hurt and abuse, the pain they have brought to others and to themselves. Heaven and hell are states of mind, of being—what we make of our lives and our world. These states start here, as we create them in ourselves, surround ourselves in their sphere, and let their influences flow through us. When we die, these states follow us because we have made them a part of us. If we have lived and grown into heavenly beings, we continue in the other life in heaven. If we have made our lives a hell, we continue in that hellish life in the other world in our own hell. This hell is not one of God's choosing, but one of our own choosing, according to our own free disposition.

Thus, God doesn't put people in heaven or hell. We put ourselves there. God created heaven as a place and a state of mind where we can be joined with him, grow with him and our fellow human beings, and experience all the joys that come from an unselfish and angelic way of life for eternity. We choose whether we want to do this or not by our choices here on earth and by our preparation for this way of life.

By the same token, hell was not created by God as a place of punishment for those who refuse his love. Think about it. What kind of God would punish people with eternal pain and hardship just because they didn't want to do what he wanted? That kind of God, as explained by one of my good friends who escaped from fundamentalism to find the New Church, "would be a playground bully. We get beat up if we don't play his way." God, being love itself, mercy itself, casts no one into hell. How could mercy do this? It can't. But God does love each one of us so much that he is willing to give us the freedom to make our own lives a hell. He gives us the freedom to do this forever, if we want to. And so hell is a spiritual place or state of mind where those go who don't want goodness or love. They don't want the light of heaven or the angelic life. In fact, if they have filled their lives and spirits with infernal delights of self-ishness, hurt, and lust, they can't stand the sphere of heaven when they get to the other world. They don't want to be near it because its heavenly atmosphere suffocates them. They want to be among their own, where they can continue in their delusions and dysfunction. It is not a happy world for those who choose hell for themselves, just as a self-serving or hurtful life in this world is not a happy one. But human beings are given the freedom to choose it, and to do so every day, so to speak, for the rest of their lives and to eternity.

The good news is that we can very easily choose a path to heaven. If only we begin to turn toward what is good, loving, and merciful, the Divine opens us up and lets the light of heaven begin to shine into us and through us. We can be lifted up. The dream, as it were, of the Divine is that all people may open up to the light and become heavenly beings, living and growing in God forever. If you want to go to heaven, don't look for any magic words or certain names of God or even confessions of certain beliefs. Just ask God to show you the way and he will. As Isaiah says, "Cease to do evil. Learn to do good. . . . Though your sins are like scarlet, they shall be like snow" (Isaiah 1:16–18), or as Jesus said, "Come to me, all you that are weary and are carrying heavy burdens, and I will give you rest. Take my yoke upon you, and learn from me; for I am gentle and humble in heart, and you will find rest for your souls" (Matthew 11:28–29). The door to heaven is open. Walk through it.

It's Real and Better Than You Thought

So often the heavenly way of life is depicted as one of sitting on a cloud, playing a harp, or beholding the glory of God forever and ever. That sounds about as boring as one can get, doesn't it? Heaven is a real place. In fact, the spiritual world has a more real feeling to it, more beauty, more clarity, more meaning, more depth, more life in it than this dense, earthly world, because it is closer to the Source, namely, to God himself. Those who have had a near-death experience confirm Swedenborg's assertions that the afterlife contains magnificent landscapes, mountains, and vistas of astounding beauty and an array of resplendent colors not seen in this world.

This beauty also extends to people, as well as wholeness and well-being. All people wake up in the other life safe and whole. Those who suffered from disease or infirmity in this world find themselves restored and healthy in the next. All grow young in heaven, restored to the springtime of their youth. Swedenborg, in talking about angelic couples growing young together in heaven, relates in *Marital Love* §137 that "wives, who now look like young women, had once been wrinkled old ladies in the world, and husbands, who now look like adolescent youths, had once been decrepit old men there. They have all been returned by the Lord to the bloom of this youthful age."

We will live in homes and communities in heaven, just like on earth. The difference is that in heaven we live in communities of people similar to ourselves. Similarity of thoughts and feelings brings togetherness quite literally in the afterlife. It is reported by Swedenborg and also by those who have had the near-death experience that approaching one's eternal destination or community, is like "coming home." In fact, when we meet the friends and neighbors in our eternal abode, we will feel as if we've know these people for all of our lives, like the closest of kin. And they are "kindred" if we think of "kindred spirits." This doesn't mean that we can't travel in heaven and meet anyone we wish to, from any time, state, or place; but we find our rest and our habitation with those who understand us and whom we understand—those with whom we can grow forever.

Heaven is also a very active place. It is not full of harpists, although I am sure there are some of those in heaven. Swedenborg calls heaven a "kingdom of uses" or useful service:

> There is no way to list all the functions that people have in the heavens or to describe them in detail, though it

is possible to say something on the subject in general terms; they are innumerable and vary depending on the roles of the communities as well. In fact, each community plays a unique role, since the communities differ depending on their virtues and therefore their function. This is because virtues for everyone in the heavens are virtues in act, which are functions. Everyone there does something specifically useful, for the Lord's kingdom is a kingdom of uses.

Heaven and Hell §387

Think about something you really love to do: maybe it is a special gift of yours, a calling, perhaps a hobby of some kind. Imagine being able to do something like this, a work that you love and that brings happiness to all who are affected by your actions in this regard. Imagine doing something that fills you with more and more delight each day and that what you do contributes to all of the heavens and earth at the same time. This is the kind of useful service you will be doing in heaven. It will involve your heart, other people, and limitless opportunities.

In the previous chapter, we learned that we will be reunited with our soul mates in an eternal marriage that combines love and wisdom. But we will meet all of our loved ones in the afterlife. We will recognize each other in the other world and celebrate that we are alive and together again. As we saw previously, married partners who learned to grow together in this world and tenderly love each other meet and congratulate each other upon their arrival. They continue together forever in heaven. It is the world of the mind and spirit. Love brings all together.

This teaching brings me comfort. I had a brother who died as a child before I was born, and I look forward to meeting him in the other world. Swedenborg says all who die as children go to heaven and tells a story of a man who lost his little brother in childhood. After a full life on earth, this man too died and entered the other world. There he met his brother who was now an angel. When Swedenborg, on one of his heavenly journeys, encountered the man, he noticed that he was crying. Swedenborg asked why. The man said that he couldn't help it. His brother spoke from so much mutual brotherly love that it was as if "love itself were speaking" (*Arcana Coelestia* §2304).

A Spatial View of the Afterlife

The afterlife, or the spiritual world, is made up of heaven, hell, and a world between the two called "the world of spirits." We first awaken in the world of spirits in the afterlife, where we undergo our final preparation for heaven or hell.

Swedenborg found that our minds are in the world of spirits right now, as we are living on earth, because we are spirits dwelling in these natural bodies, although we are not aware of this "other" world. Carl Jung, who read Swedenborg extensively, calls this world the "collective unconsciousness" where all touch each other and affect each other on a spiritual level. The spiritual influences that manifest themselves to us in every waking moment of the day, that is, the impulses behind the thoughts and feelings we experience, come from associations with this world. When we die, we become conscious of this world of spirits and dwell fully within it.

As we become familiar and comfortable with this new world, we begin to gravitate to those who are most like us and with whom we find common companionship. This likeness is not a matter of race, nationality, or creed, but based solely on our hearts, on what we hold most dear. Eventually we make our way to our eternal homes in heaven or hell, as we become, so to speak, refined or centered in what we truly wish to be to eternity. These three worlds are alluded to by Jesus in his parable of the rich man and Lazarus who end up in hell and in heaven, respectively; we are told that there is a "great chasm" between these two worlds (see Luke 16:26).

There are also different depths or levels to heaven and to hell, according to the depth of goodness or evil in each individual and in the collective societies. The purest and most loving angels are at a higher, more interior level of heaven than those of a lesser goodness and development of love and wisdom. Lower hells are reserved for the more diabolical and hurtful. And so Paul speaks of the "third heaven" (II Corinthians 12:2), and the Old Testament speaks of the "lowest hell" (Deuteronomy 32:22). We are situated in the spiritual world according to our relationship with God. If we have pushed God away from our lives, along with his love and blessings, we find ourselves dwelling far away from God's manifest presence in the afterlife. We are never completely removed from God, in his mercy, but we can "go very low," to use a familiar phrase. Those who are close to God in heart and life live closer to God in heaven. This only makes sense. If you're close to God, you're close to God literally in heaven.

What Swedenborg Learned about Heaven

People who have had a near-death experience speak of seeing a being of pure light, which doesn't hurt their eyes but rather radiates wisdom and love. Swedenborg also wrote about this in his description of heaven, calling this light the "spiritual sun," saying that this is the usual way God appears before angels. Imagine the beautiful light of heaven shining down upon you and that light is God's love and wisdom, filling you with warmth, love, knowledge, and understanding. This light is always shining at about a 45-degree angle in the sky, in front of all. And so, when Jesus was talking of the angels with children, he remarked, "Take care that you do not despise one of these little ones; for, I tell you, in heaven their angels continually see the face of my Father in heaven" (Matthew 18:10).

Just as the spiritual sun is constant, each angel has a role that he or she fulfills throughout eternity. Everyone in heaven performs some function that helps all others. It's similar to how each part of a human body functions in perfect connection with all others to keep the body healthy and running in top condition. In fact, each person's useful contribution is related to the function of the greater body of the whole. Some play the heart of this body, some the mind, some the arms, legs, all the many organs and senses. Swedenborg says that, in God's eyes, all of the heavens appear as one person, with each individual playing a role in making that person beautiful and perfect. He calls it the Universal Human or the Grand Man.

Heaven really is a place of peace, growth, and joy. Our happiness grows each day as we learn to love more and more with every new opportunity. We are free from the struggle between good and evil that we endure on earth. We are free from the doubts that accompany temptation and strife. We are free of the pain that comes from the hurt we cause ourselves in our misguided escapades or the hurt that others may cause us. Heaven is a wonderful place!

> The divine quality of peace in heaven comes from the Lord, arising from his union with heaven's angels, and specifically from the union of the good and the true within each angel. These are the sources of peace. Peace in the heavens is the divine nature intimately affecting everything good there with blessedness.
>
> *Heaven and Hell* §286

That peace is like the morning time or dawn in spring, when, once the night is passed, all things of earth begin to take new life from the rising sun; the dew that falls from heaven spreads a leafy fragrance far and wide, and springtime's gentle warmth makes meadows fertile and instills its charm in human minds as well.

Heaven and Hell §289

We may gather the magnitude of heaven's pleasure simply from the fact that for everyone there it is delightful to share their pleasure and bliss with someone else; and since everyone in the heavens is like this, we can see how immense heaven's pleasure is. For there is in heaven a sharing by everyone with each individual, and by each individual with everyone.

Heaven and Hell §399

Jesus said, "Peace I leave with you; my peace I give to you. I do not give to you as the world gives. Do not let your hearts be troubled, and do not let them be afraid. . . . I have said these things to you so that my joy may be in you, and that your joy may be complete. This is my commandment, that you love one another as I have loved you" (John 14:27; 15:11–12). Heaven is available to all of us, regardless of our faith, background, or past. Heaven is a state of the heart and soul. Heaven is love. If we believe in heaven and want this as our happy eternal abode, then we should turn from evil, learn to do good, and love. If we do this and learn to love truly, we will enter the joy of our Creator. As it is stated in Matthew 25:23, we will hear, "Well done, good and faithful servant; you have been trustworthy in a few things, I will put you in charge of many things; enter into the joy of your master."

8

Are We Living In The End Times?

Relax! It's not the end of the world. Some religious groups put a great deal of emphasis on the Apocalypse. They use scare tactics, telling people that they have to get ready now, that God is coming at any moment with his wrath and fury, that they had better get on the right side and batten down the hatches because here comes Armageddon.

Relax! God isn't going to blow up the world he created. He isn't interested in destroying humankind or ruining our ecology by lakes of fire or nasty plagues and earthquakes and such. God loves us. Our world will last as long as our sun continues to shine and as long as we don't destroy it. But God will never destroy our earth or the people on it.

Certainly, Jesus spoke of a Second Coming. He did talk about a lot of destruction. But notice what he says, "And you will hear of wars and rumors of wars; see that you are not alarmed; for this must take place, but the end is not yet. For nation will rise against nation, and kingdom against kingdom, and there will be famines and earthquakes in various places: all this is but the beginning of the birth pangs" (Matthew 24:6–8). Notice that these calamities happen all the time on this earth with every generation. Jesus must be speaking of something deeper and something more spiritual than things blowing up and falling apart and people fighting one another. In fact, Jesus goes on to say, "Immediately after the suffering of those days the sun will be darkened, and the moon will not give its light; the stars will fall from heaven, and the powers of the heavens will be shaken. Then the sign of the Son of Man will appear in heaven, and then all the tribes of the earth will mourn, and they will see 'the Son of Man coming on the clouds of heaven' with power and great glory" (Matthew 24:29–30). Notice here that there will be no sun or moon anymore, but somehow the earth will still be here. Notice that the stars are going to fall, but fall to where? Stars are suns and planets. How will Jesus come on clouds without any atmosphere because the universe has van-ished? In other words, how could anyone even think that these words of Jesus are to be taken literally? He is speaking figuratively.

A New Advent

Swedenborg deciphered the hidden meaning behind the biblical description of the Second Coming. The Second Coming of Christ is not some cataclysmic end of the world as we know it; rather it is something spiritual. The sun and the moon symbolize our human love and faith, as in the Creation story. Jesus says that love will begin to fade and faith with it. Stars are all the wonderful insights that humankind enjoys when connected to God. Disconnected, they fall from our consciousness as stars from the sky. The dark time for humanity when Jesus predicts he will come again is dark in spirit, not dark from lack of natural light. People will turn away from love and faith, fight each other, starve for goodness and truth in their lives, and struggle to connect with God. The promise of Jesus is that, when this time comes, he will not abandon us, that he will make his presence known. Coming in the clouds of heaven means revealing himself in the literal stories of his own Word, as a visible, understandable God. In the New Church, we believe that Jesus' Second Coming is the development of a new understanding of and relationship with the Lord, the dawn of a new era of believing, loving, and living.

Doesn't that make more sense? Jesus isn't going to come and destroy the world. Rather, he comes to bring a new and deeper understanding of who he is and what a life in his ways is all about. And as this understanding grows, so the coming of the Lord reaches its fullness. Jesus said to his disciples, "I still have many things to say to you, but you cannot bear them now. When the Spirit of truth comes, he will guide you into all the truth; for he will not speak on his own, but will speak whatever he hears, and he will declare to you the things that are to come. He will glorify me, because he will take what is mine and declare it to you" (John 16:12–14). I personally believe that Swe-denborg's teachings are God-given and that they are a vessel of the "Spirit of truth" in the sense that Swedenborg's teachings have "glorified" Jesus as the one God of heaven and earth and that he has certainly taken "what is [Jesus'] and declared it" to us.

Since Swedenborg's time, a new dawn of spiritual freedom has emerged on earth. The dignity of human beings of all races and colors has been made known and begun to be respected and honored as never before. Slavery, for instance, has been outlawed (Swedenborgians were involved in that fight both in Europe and America). Organized religion, in its worst state of abuse, no longer holds the same power of mind-control over others that it used to in times of inquisitions, castigations, and robbery of the poor in the name of God. The back of such monstrous spiritual tyranny has been broken. So, in speaking of this new advent, Swedenborg says the following in *The Last Judgment and Babylon Destroyed* §§73–74:

> The future state of the world will be exactly the same as it has been up to now; for the mighty change which has taken place in the spiritual world does not cause any change in the external appearance of the natural

world. So just as before there will be politics, peace-treaties, alliances and wars, and all other . . . features of society. . . . The future state of the church, however, will not be the same. It may seem much the same in outward appearance, but inwardly it will be different. In outward appearance churches will be divided from one another as before, their teachings will differ as before, and so will the religious systems of the Gentiles. But people in the church will, from now on, have more freedom in thinking about matters of faith, and so about the spiritual matters of heaven, because spiritual freedom has been restored. . . . The slavery and captivity in which people of the church up to now have been held, has been taken away.

A New Jerusalem

At the end of the book of Revelation, the Apostle John witnesses the descent of the Holy City, the New Jerusalem, coming down from heaven to the earth, prepared as a bride adorned for her husband. He says that this city shall have no need of the light of the sun, for God himself will be that light. There will be gates on every side of the city. All with pure hearts will be welcomed there. In that city there will be no death, sorrow, or crying, no more pain. In the middle of that city will be a beautiful river, clear as crystal, and a tree called "the tree of life" whose leaves will be for the healing of the nations. Here God will dwell with his people and they with him.

This beautiful vision is of a new church. It isn't necessarily one organized body, but rather a new fellowship of believers who, from every faith, will turn to God and follow his ways. This is an image of the human race, as it comes to accept the divinity and humanity of God, and a life in the ways of God.

The gates of the city symbolize all the different ways people will approach God and find their way to recognizing him in his human form as the Lord Jesus Christ, not just in name, but personally in life. The light that shines in that city is the enlightenment and understanding of life that will come to all who explore this city in the teachings of the New Church, about genuine and living faith, charity, mercy, and love. There will be no more spiritual death for those who enter that city, or way of life, no more emptiness, coldness of heart, joyless existence of evil, but rather peace, confidence, and joy. The promise is that those who are willing to become spiritual will one day cease from feeling the pain of temptation, the sorrow of spiritual failure and loss. God "will wipe every tear from their eyes" (Rev. 21:4). The river of life is God's Word newly revealed. The leaves of the tree of life are all the common-sense matters of belief that will be spread to all faiths and walks of life, as healing medicine. The knowledge that God is pure love, that all providence works for our happiness and salvation, that it's never too late to find the path to God, that no one really dies but lives forever, that anyone can be free from the pain of self-ishness and want, that love between two people never dies, that we human beings are more than the stuff that stars are made of because we were created in the image of God and have been given the freedom to fill ourselves with and radiate that love and wisdom from the Divine as much as we desire—all of these truths are the healing medicine for all people of the world, beginning with us. And so Jesus says at the end of the prophecy of the New Church in the book of Revelation, "See, I am making all things new. . . It is done! I am the Alpha and the Omega, the beginning and the end. To the thirsty I will give water as a gift from the spring of the water of life. Those who conquer will inherit these things, and I will be their God and they will be my children" (Rev 21:5–7). This is the promise of the New Church. We must find in our hearts the answer given by John himself, at the end of the book of Revelation. When Jesus says, "Surely I am coming soon" (Rev. 22:20), his response is simple and humble: "Amen. Come, Lord Jesus!" (Rev. 22:21).

9

You Can Believe!

You can believe! You can believe in a God who will never let you down. This God created you out of pure love and will love you not only for the rest of your life, but for eternity. He is both divine and human. He is all-powerful and all-merci-ful, too. He reaches out to you with open arms, inviting you into his embrace. His name is Jesus Christ. He is a gentle shep-herd, a healer, teacher, leader, mentor, even friend. He is not far away, but right here with you. Jesus said, "Remember, I am with you always" (Matthew 28:20). You can know him, under-stand him, trust him, love him, and have a continually growing relationship with him. And he doesn't just love you or one group of people who know him by this name. He loves every-one. He loves Jews and Gentiles, Hindus, Muslims, people from all different cultures and lands! But we need to open our-selves up to his love, by turning away from evil and learning to love what is good. God looks at the heart, because he is Heart. He can enter inside and dwell with those who learn to love, be-cause he is Love. Jesus said, "Listen! I am standing at the door, knocking; if you hear my voice and open the door, I will come in to you and eat with you, and you with me" (Rev. 3:20).

You can believe in yourself. You are not inherently evil or good, although you can choose to become either one. You are free. You are free to choose the path set out before you, free to fulfill your potential and God's wondrous dream for you. You are a child of God with the potential for incredible greatness.

God created you for a purpose, as a gift to the rest of us. What you choose to become and to do with your life makes a huge difference to this world. In *Arcana Coelestia* §3854, Swedenborg stated, "For every smallest fraction of a moment of a person's life entails a chain of consequences extending into eternity. Indeed every one is like a new beginning to those that follow, and so every single moment of the life both of his understanding and of his will is a new beginning." Make those moments count. Make your life a giveaway. Give that love away, that God-given talent, that certain something that is you that no one else has. Let it shine through. That's part of being a spiritual person, and it's fun. It's joyful.

Life itself is a process, an incredible journey. The journey isn't completed in a moment, an hour, or a day. It is a lifetime of trial and error, of difficult passages and exhilarating breakthroughs. I find comfort in knowing that this journey has its tough moments as well as its peak experiences. Why? Because I already know this from experience and can rest assured that I am not unique in my trials of life, and I know that God knows what I am going through and cares. When God sent the Israelites manna in the wilderness, bread from heaven for their nourishment, he told them only to collect enough for that day. That bread symbolizes the good things we receive from God each day, all our happiness. It is our daily bread for which we pray. When we look to God each day, we are living one day at a time. Throughout each new day of our journey, God is there to feed us. As the Psalmist says to God, "The eyes of all look to you, and you give them their food in due season. You open your hand, satisfying the desire of every living thing" (Psalm 145:15–16). God will care for us, give us what we need, will bless us.

Can you take the mature approach to your spiritual growth by committing to the whole journey, turning your will and your life over to God each day? You can, one day at a time. In your quest for spirituality, you need an authority greater than self to look to as a guide. In this way, we have an opportunity to reach for something greater than ourselves. I'm not talking about adopting a person as a guide, but rather adopting a way of living. There are many good books and philosophies on how to live life to the fullest. I recommend that you read as many as you can and obtain a sense of what is available out there. But more than anything else, I recommend that the Bible be the devotional book for daily reading. In *The Doctrine of the Sacred Scripture* §78, Swedenborg says, "It is through the Word that the Lord is present with a person and is united with a person, for the Lord is the Word, and as it were speaks with the person in it." The Gospel of John begins with these words, "In the beginning was the Word, and the Word was with God, and the Word was God" (John 1:1). The truth contained in God's Word is unlimited, just as God is unlimited. When you approach this sacred book, do so with an open mind and heart, and ask to be shown the truth and to experience the deeper levels of truth that this book has to offer. The Bible is a parable about you, and you can learn more about the inner meanings of each story in God's Word and learn about your life, about the secrets of heaven, as described in the writings of Emanuel Swedenborg.

Your life is eternal. Your love is eternal. Your relationships that are based on love are eternal. Keep this in mind as you explore your world each day. Look for the higher meaning, and strive for the higher goal. It will open up a new reality to you. You will sense the hand of providence in your friendships, in your marriage. You can grow so much more and on so many deeper levels with this eternal view. Life is forever. Take the long view. See what it brings. The gifts are amazing and enduring.

Sometimes it can seem a difficult task to adopt a spiritual way of life, and not only learn to believe in God and heaven, but to live a new life according to that belief. The truth is that we can't do it ourselves. The very nature of spirituality contains within it the recognition that the Divine is the source of our strength, or love, our very life. This knowledge is itself a gift, to learn and to know that, whoever we are or whatever our condition may be, we can be lifted up. We can be set on a path that leads to all things beautiful, and we never have to walk that path alone again. We can and will be guided to fulfill our dreams, and God's dream for us, that we may be filled with the joy love brings, as we become willing participants of that love.

Take that first step. God will take care of you for the rest of the way.

Who Was
Emanuel Swedenborg?[1]

E manuel Swedenborg was an eighteenth-century scientist who was well known and respected in his time for his scientific accomplishments. Having experienced a major spiritual awakening, he began to write books about the nature of God, the spiritual life, heaven and hell, a deeper meaning to the Bible, providence, marriage, and the Second Coming of Christ. He believed that his teachings were divinely inspired and that they would be the foundation for the rebirth of Christianity.

Born in Stockholm, on January 29, 1688, the son of a clergyman and professor of theology, Swedenborg grew up in a household filled with moral, political, intellectual, and philosophical dialogue. After his formal education at Uppsala University, at the age of twenty-two, Swedenborg began to travel. While in England and Holland, he immersed himself in studying many subjects, including physics, astronomy, mathematics, anatomy, physiology, economics, metallurgy, mineralogy, geology, chemistry, watch-making, bookbinding, and lens grinding.

During this time of travel and scholarship, Swedenborg began his career of public service. In 1716, the king of Sweden

---

1. This biographical synopsis was written by Mac Frazier and edited by Grant Schnarr. For a more complete, brief biography of Emanuel Swedenborg, see *A Scientist Explores Spirit* by George Dole and Robert Kirven (West Chester, Pa.: Chrysalis Books, 1997).

appointed young Swedenborg as extraordinary assessor in the Royal College of Mines. Then, in 1719, he took a seat in the House of Nobles (a part of the Swedish legislature), in which he served the Swedish government for some fifty years. The king, impressed with Swedenborg's contributions as editor of *Daedalus Hyperboreus* (a periodical dedicated to the discussion of natural sciences), asked Swedenborg to serve as his engineering advisor. In that capacity, Swedenborg devised numerous feats of engineering to aid the military and industry. He also planned and designed many inventions. Although most were never built, they included a submarine, an airplane, a steam engine, an air gun, and a slow-combustion stove.

Befitting a man of his intellectual strength and fervor, Swedenborg published many books on a vast number of subjects. Two subjects that he made particular advances in were metallurgy and biology. Especially impressive is the work he did in connection with the nervous system; he is generally credited with being the first to understand the significance of the cerebral cortex and the respiratory movement of the brain tissues.

As a philosopher, however, Swedenborg wasn't satisfied with a purely physical approach to studying humanity and the universe. In particular, his ambition was to comprehend more fully the nature of the soul and to develop a new, more accurate cosmology than had ever before been proposed. Based upon his conviction that underlying all matter in the universe was divine force, he wrote of the relationships between matter and energy, between the finite and the infinite, and between God and humanity.

Then, in 1744, his life took an unexpected turn. He began to have vivid, disturbing, and exhilarating dreams and visions. Not knowing what to make of these odd experiences, he revealed them nowhere but in his personal journals. Moved partially by the need to understand his own recent experiences and partially by the direction his studies in cosmology and the human soul were taking, he began a meticulous study of the Bible.

In April 1745, Emanuel Swedenborg had an experience that forever changed his life. The Lord appeared to him and told him something amazing: a human person was needed to serve as the means by which God would further reveal himself to humanity, somewhat in the manner of the biblical visions of the Old Testament. So began Swedenborg's life as a spiritual revelator.

From then until his death in 1772, Swedenborg studied the Bible, perfected his knowledge of Hebrew and Greek, and wrote numerous theological works that have become the foundation for the New Church. Throughout this time, confirming what the Lord was revealing to him, he was in periodic communication with spirits in heaven and in hell—exploring all the wonders of the world to come. In numerous books, he revealed the hidden, inner meaning to the stories of the Old and New Testaments; the fundamental nature of God, humanity, and creation; the truth about the afterlife; the keys to our own personal spiritual growth; the real meaning of the Book of Revelation; and the beautiful inner secrets behind true loving marriages, just to name a few things.

At first, his books went largely unnoticed. He published them anonymously at his own cost, sending them to the learned people of his day, but the general public was still unaware of his newfound discoveries. This began to change after a strange occurrence in July of 1759. Swedenborg was in Gothenburg, Sweden, dining with friends at the home of a wealthy local merchant. During the dinner, he suddenly became distraught and withdrew from the table. When asked what was the matter, he replied that he had just had news that a horrible fire had broken out in Stockholm (which was 300 miles from Gothenburg), not far from his own home. Then, at around eight o'clock that same evening, he just as suddenly became relieved, explaining that the fire had been extinguished three houses down from his own home.

His words and behavior of that evening became the talk of the town just a few days later, when a messenger arrived from Stockholm with news about the fire Swedenborg had described. Upon questioning, it was discovered that his description of the event had perfectly matched, in much detail, what had actually happened that summer evening. Soon afterward, the first surge of interest in his theological writings began, spurred on not only by the strange story of his uncanny knowledge of the Stockholm fire, but also by several other episodes that demonstrated his ability to communicate with people in the spiritual world.

For the remainder of his life, Swedenborg continued to visit the other world and publish books revealing what he believed God had summoned him to write. He also maintained an active life in this world, taking part in political discussions in the Swedish House of Lords and writing on such diverse topics as Sweden's monetary policy and how to inlay marble tables. Then, on Sunday, March 29, 1772, at five o'clock in the afternoon, Emanuel Swedenborg entered into the spiritual world for the final time, never to return again (incidentally, dying exactly when he had earlier predicted he would).

Since his death, his writings have affected thousands of people, both directly and indirectly. The universal theology put forth in his works has contributed to advancement of religious thought all across the world, from Christianity to Buddhism, and has inspired many great persons, including Ralph Waldo Emerson, Helen Keller, Johnny "Appleseed" Chapman . . . the list goes on and on. Most importantly, the writings of Emanuel Swedenborg have served as the foundation for a new Christian Church, which is growing all over the world.

Bibliography Of Works By Emanuel Swedenborg

Apocalypse Explained. 6 vols. Translated by John Whitehead. 2nd ed. West Chester, Pa.: The Swedenborg Foundation, 1994–1998.

Apocalypse Revealed. 2 vols. Translated by John Whitehead. 2nd ed. West Chester, Pa.: The Swedenborg Foundation, 1997.
  A new translation of this work, to be entitled *Revelation Unveiled*, will be available from the NEW CENTURY EDITION OF THE WORKS OF EMANUEL SWEDENBORG in the near future.

Arcana Coelestia. 12 vols. Translated by John Clowes. Revised by John F. Potts. 2nd ed. West Chester, Pa.: The Swedenborg Foundation, 1995–1998. The first volume of this work is also available under the title *Heavenly Secrets*.
  A new translation of this work, to be entitled *Secrets of Heaven*, will be available from the NEW CENTURY EDITION OF THE WORKS OF EMANUEL SWEDENBORG in the near future.

Charity: The Practice of Neighborliness. Translated by William F. Wunsch. Edited by William R. Woofenden. West Chester, Pa.: The Swedenborg Foundation, 1995.

Conjugial Love. Translated by Samuel S. Warren. Revised by
    Louis Tafel. 2nd ed. West Chester, Pa.: The
    Swedenborg Foundation, 1998. This volume is also
    available under the title *Love in Marriage*, translated by
    David Gladish, 1992.
        A new translation of this work, to be entitled
    Marriage Love, will be available from the **New
    Century Edition of the Works of Emanuel
    Swedenborg** in the near future.

Divine Love and Wisdom. Translated by John C. Ager. 2nd ed.
    West Chester, Pa.: The Swedenborg Foundation, 1995.

Divine Love and Wisdom/Divine Providence. Translated by
    George F. Dole. **The New Century Edition of
    the Works of Emanuel Swedenborg.** West
    Chester, Pa.: The Swedenborg Foundation, 2003.

Divine Providence. Translated by William Wunsch. 2nd ed.
    West Chester, Pa.: The Swedenborg Foundation, 1996.

Four Doctrines. Translated by John F. Potts. 2nd ed. West
    Chester, Pa.: The Swedenborg Foundation, 1997.
        A new translation of the individual volumes of
    this collection—*The Lord, Sacred Scripture, Life,* and
    Faith—will be available from the **New Century
    Edition of the Works of Emanuel Swedenborg**
    in the near future.

Heaven and Hell. Translated by John C. Ager. 2nd ed. West
    Chester, Pa.: The Swedenborg Foundation, 1995.

———. Translated by George F. Dole. THE NEW CENTURY EDITION OF THE WORKS OF EMANUEL SWEDENBORG. West Chester, Pa.: The Swedenborg Foundation, 2000.

The Heavenly City. Translated by Lee Woofenden. West Chester, Pa.: The Swedenborg Foundation, 1993. See also *The New Jerusalem and Its Heavenly Doctrine,* below.

Journal of Dreams. Translated by J. J. G. Wilkinson. Introduction by Wilson Van Dusen. New York: The Swedenborg Foundation, 1986. See also *Swedenborg's Dream Diary.*

The Last Judgment in Retrospect. Translated and edited by George F. Dole. West Chester, Pa.: The Swedenborg Foundation, 1996. See also *The Last Judgment and Babylon Destroyed.*

Miscellaneous Theological Works. Translated by John Whitehead. 2nd ed. West Chester, Pa.: The Swedenborg Foundation, 1996. This volume includes *The New Jerusalem and Its Heavenly Doctrine, Earths in the Universe,* and *The Last Judgment and Babylon Destroyed,* among others.

New translations of the individual titles in this collection will be available from the NEW CENTURY EDITION OF THE WORKS OF EMANUEL SWEDENBORG in the near future.

Posthumous Theological Works. 2 vols. Translated by John Whitehead. 2nd ed. West Chester, Pa.: The Swedenborg Foundation, 1996. These volumes include autobiographical and theological extracts from

Swedenborg's letters, *Additions to True Christian Religion, The Doctrine of Charity, The Precepts of the Decalogue*, and collected minor works, among others.

Swedenborg's Dream Diary. Edited by Lars Bergquist. Translated by Anders Hallengren. West Chester, Pa.: The Swedenborg Foundation, 2001. See also *Journal of Dreams*.

True Christian Religion. 2 vols. Translated by John C. Ager. 2nd ed. West Chester, Pa.: The Swedenborg Foundation, 1996.

True Christianity. 2 vols. Translated by Jonathan Rose. THE NEW CENTURY EDITION OF THE WORKS OF EMANUEL SWEDENBORG. West Chester, Pa.: The Swedenborg Foundation, forthcoming.

Worship and Love of God. Translated by Alfred H. Stroh and Frank Sewall. 2nd ed. West Chester, Pa.: The Swedenborg Foundation, 1996.

————. Translated by Stuart Shotwell. THE NEW CENTURY EDITION OF THE WORKS OF EMANUEL SWEDENBORG. West Chester, Pa.: The Swedenborg Foundation, forthcoming.

Collections of Swedenborg's Writings

A Compendium of the Theological Writings of Emanuel Swedenborg. Translated and edited by Samuel S. Warren. 1875; rpt. New York: Swedenborg Foundation, 1974.

Conversations with Angels: What Swedenborg Heard in Heaven. Edited by Leonard Fox and Donald Rose. Translated by David Gladish and Jonathan Rose. West Chester, Pa.: Chrysalis Books, 1996.

Debates with Devils: What Swedenborg Heard in Hell. Edited by Donald Rose. Translated by Lisa Hyatt Cooper. West Chester, Pa.: Chrysalis Books, 2000.

Essential Swedenborg. Edited by Sig Synnestvedt. Rpt. West Chester, Pa.: The Swedenborg Foundation, 1977.

Poems from Swedenborg. Edited by Leon C. Le Van. New York: The Swedenborg Foundation, 1987.

A Thoughtful Soul. Translated and edited by George F. Dole. West Chester, Pa.: Chrysalis Books, 1995.

Way of Wisdom: Meditations on Love and Service. Edited by Grant R. Schnarr and Erik J. Buss. West Chester, Pa.: Chrysalis Books, 1999.

Works by Grant Schnarr

Art of Spiritual Warfare: A Guide to Lasting Inner Peace Based on Sun Tzu's The Art of War. Wheaton, Ill.: Theosophical Publishing House, 2000.

Way of Wisdom: Meditations on Love and Service. Edited by Grant R. Schnarr and Erik J. Buss. West Chester, Pa.: Chrysalis Books, 1999.

Spiritual Recovery: A Twelve-Step Guide. West Chester, Pa.: Chrysalis Books, 1998

Return to the Promised Land: The Story of Our Spiritual Recovery. West Chester, Pa.: Chrysalis Books, 1997.

About The Author

Grant Schnarr is an author, teacher, certified life-coach, and assistant pastor of the Bryn Athyn Church in Bryn Athyn, Pennsylvania. He is the author of several books on spiritual growth and recovery; his recent work *The Art of Spiritual Warfare* has been published in several languages on four continents. He and his wife Cathy are the parents of four grown sons.

You can learn more about Grant Schnarr at his website: www.spiritual-recovery.com.

Other titles by Grant Schnarr

Return to the Promised Land
The Story of Our Spiritual Recovery

This guide book for spiritual recovery compares the Israelites' biblical struggles in the wilderness to our own life crises. Practical, twelve-step exercises help the reader escape destructive behaviors.

4, pb, $12.95

e seeking spiritual n the 'fury of inner o lasting peace."

rs Weekly

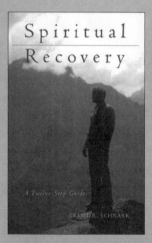

Spiritual Recovery
A Twelve-Step Guide

Twelve-step programs, based on psychological and spiritual development, serve all who desire spiritual growth. Using a twelve-step approach, Grand Schnarr opens a path to freedom, away from destructive tendencies, toward a deeper relationship with God and self.

0-87785-379-7, pb, $13.95

"Schnarr listens to the heart and discounts irrelevant dogmas."—*Publishers Weekly*

Swedenborg Foundation Publishers / Chrysalis Books
(800) 355-3222, ext. 10
customerservice@swedenborg.com • www.swedenborg.com